COMPRESSION

STEVEN HOLL

Princeton Architectural Press New York

For Dimitra Tsachrelia and Io Helene Holl

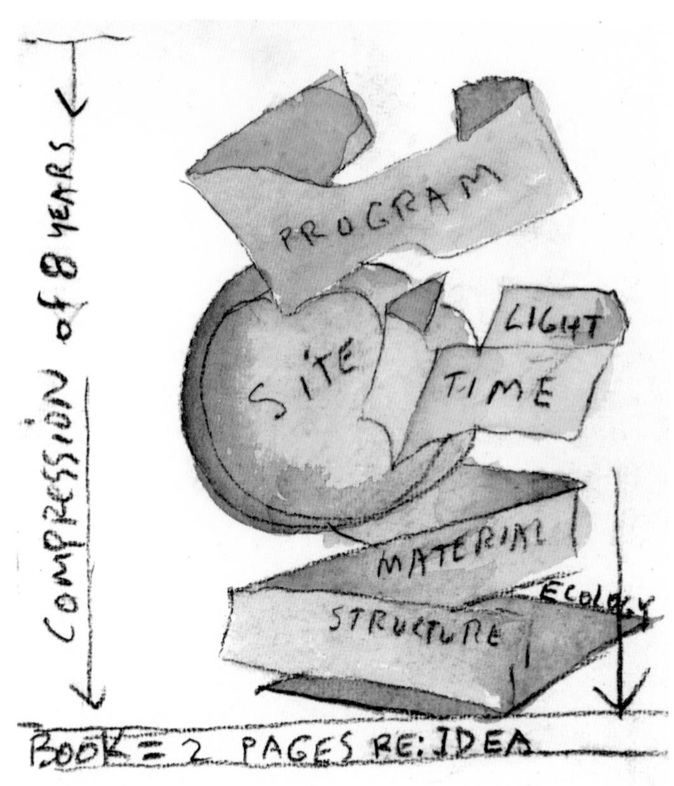
COMPRESSION of 8 YEARS
PROGRAM
SITE
LIGHT
TIME
MATERIAL
ECOLOGY
STRUCTURE
BOOK = 2 PAGES RE: IDEA

FOREWORD

On July 25, 2018, I spent an afternoon with Álvaro Siza in his office in Porto, Portugal. I had agreed to give the summer lecture at the Porto Academy if I could have five minutes with Siza. I feel that at eighty-five, he is the greatest living architect—and more than anything, architecture takes time.

In our office the average duration from first sketch to opening ceremony is eight years. I remember attending a reading by Jorge Luis Borges at the 92nd Street Y in New York in the early 1980s. If I remember correctly, he said he did not believe in infinite space. For him, the infinite was time. (Living in Manhattan is a gift. I have heard readings by Octavio Paz and Borges—both twice.)

Recently, while crossing time zones at thirty-three thousand feet in the air, I reread *Time Regained*, the final volume of Marcel Proust's *In Search of Lost Time*. Proust writes of the "purely mental character of reality." In literature, as in architecture, "it is not individuals who really exist and are in consequence capable of being expressed, but ideas."

Compression condenses selected works from the last ten years. This is the fifth volume, all by Princeton Architectural Press, in the same format, following *Anchoring* (1989), *Intertwining* (1996), *House* (2007), and *Urbanisms* (2009).

Anchoring focused on ideas such as the universal in the specific. I fondly remember my lecture at the book's launch, which accompanied an exhibition of my work at the Museum of Modern Art in New York. As a forty-one-year-old (unknown) architect, I stood at the podium of the museum's auditorium, describing my projects—only three had been built. Now, twenty-nine years have passed, and we have realized sixty works of architecture.

Without epistemological shifts, our work has continued to center around the core concerns laid out in *Anchoring*:

SITE: the universal in the specific;
IDEA: limited concept, phenomena of light and space, urban porosity;
PARALLAX: the body moving through space;
MATERIAL AND DETAIL: the haptic realm.

We have limited the size of our office and turned down several developer projects. Being selective has kept our atelier inspired to set the bar high and aim for idea-driven, quality work.

We are deeply grateful to all those who have dedicated long hours in the struggle to realize qualities in immeasurable space.

The video links following projects expand on the ideas compressed in this book.

Steven Holl
Rhinebeck, New York
October 2018

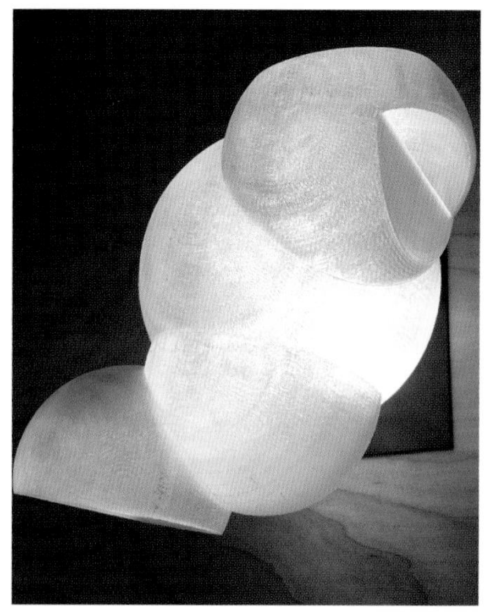

1.

2.

3.

COMPRESSION

The compression of a manifold of things into a few is at the core of poetry. What are the ideas of compression in architecture?

Compression, or densification, is one of our ideals in architecture: the condensation of a manifold of requirements—program, site, space, light, details—via a concept that yields exhilarating experiential phenomena. The reducible properties in architecture are all the things we must deal with daily: How much does it cost? How green is the building? How inventive is it? These are valid subjects, but do we also question whether there is a core of value that is intense enough? Architecture aims, through cognition via concept, toward a meaning inseparable from its space, form, and material.

For example, our 915-square-foot (85-square-meter) Ex of IN House, a little building that began in the "Explorations of IN" studies inspired by Peter Sloterdijk's research into "metaphorical implications of spherical forms," was developed in many concept models that led to the realized house. As first a spatial experiment in natural light, the house is geothermally and solar powered, with all details such as windows, doors, and printed light fixtures invented.

Even smaller is the 450-square-foot (42-square-meter) Editions de Parfums Frédéric Malle we realized in 2014 at 94 Greenwich Avenue in Manhattan. Here, the olfactory experience was imagined as "slipped disk" geometry (a circle sliced and shifted, like human olfactory receptors) realized in foamed aluminum, natural walnut, and custom cast-bronze door pulls.

The term *compression* also refers to larger social aspirations, as in the shaping of social condensers. We use it to express the aim of activating interior or exterior spaces to add to public space in our time of increased privatization. However, what we want to convey is not literal. Tension, a kind

4.

5.

of elasticity, is at the essence of thought. The greater the tension, the greater the potential.

Creative work is the compression of ideas in tension, testing limits.

In the physical realm, compression is the result of materials dislocating under compressive stress. In data compression, it's the process of encoding information digitally using fewer and fewer bits. In gas compression, volume is reduced and pressure is increased. In geology, the volume of rocks is decreased.

Architecture has the power to put essence back into day-to-day existence. Instead of focusing on the fewer and fewer bits of the one-way digital compressive process, the beautiful details of the omitted gray zones are celebrated.

Ripples of projected sunlight on a white ceiling, the naked magic of gray daylight felt as vapor, immeasurable space...The focus of compression yields the irreducible and the ineffable: a truth in the details.

1.
Cornstarch-based, CNC-printed light fixtures, Ex of IN House, Rhinebeck, New York

2. and 4.
Bronze door-pull detail, Editions de Parfums Frédéric Malle, New York, New York

3.
Fountain, Editions de Parfums Frédéric Malle, New York, New York

5.
Door pull, Herning Museum of Contemporary Art, Herning, Denmark

We shape our buildings, and afterwards our buildings shape us.
—WINSTON CHURCHILL

THINKING

1. ARCHITECTURE: ACTIVATING THE BRAIN

Architecture does not exist, what exists is the spirit of Architecture.
—LOUIS KAHN

I presented this topic in a lecture on September 25, 2016, at the Salk Institute for Biological Studies in La Jolla, California. Also speaking was the great brain scientist Eric Kandel, MD, who had just published *Reductionism in Art and Brain Science*. Kandel argues, via neuroscience, that the brain needs abstraction.

The internal mechanisms with which we see and experience visual and physical phenomena depend on a bottom-up approach—building up from elements of abstraction. The opposite, top-down approach of given figuration stifles necessary imagination.

This idea that the mind needs abstraction to throw open the range of its thought capacity is a fundamental parallel to art and architecture.

The reverie of light and space of an inspiring room, the glossy surface of plaster against stone, the flicker of sunlight on water are abstract in essence.

Certain authentic material and spatial presences reveal an essentially abstract mental image. Our imagination is set in motion and with curiosity leads to enthusiasm for multiple interpretations.

From a room to a house to a street to a city, abstract thought is like Aristotelian form—form giving cause. We might recall, on a cosmic scale, the noosphere, or sphere of unified consciousness, imagined in 1922 by Pierre Teilhard de Chardin—an abstract vision that is reflected in our internet reality today.

Today's microsecond global communication, with its image capacities, sets us in an unprecedented context. Distance has collapsed in flash communication—unique in Earth's history. We can instantaneously reflect on the fragile planet we share, and we also hold amazing tools with the potential to alter our fragile environment.

opposite
Louis Kahn, Salk Institute, 1965

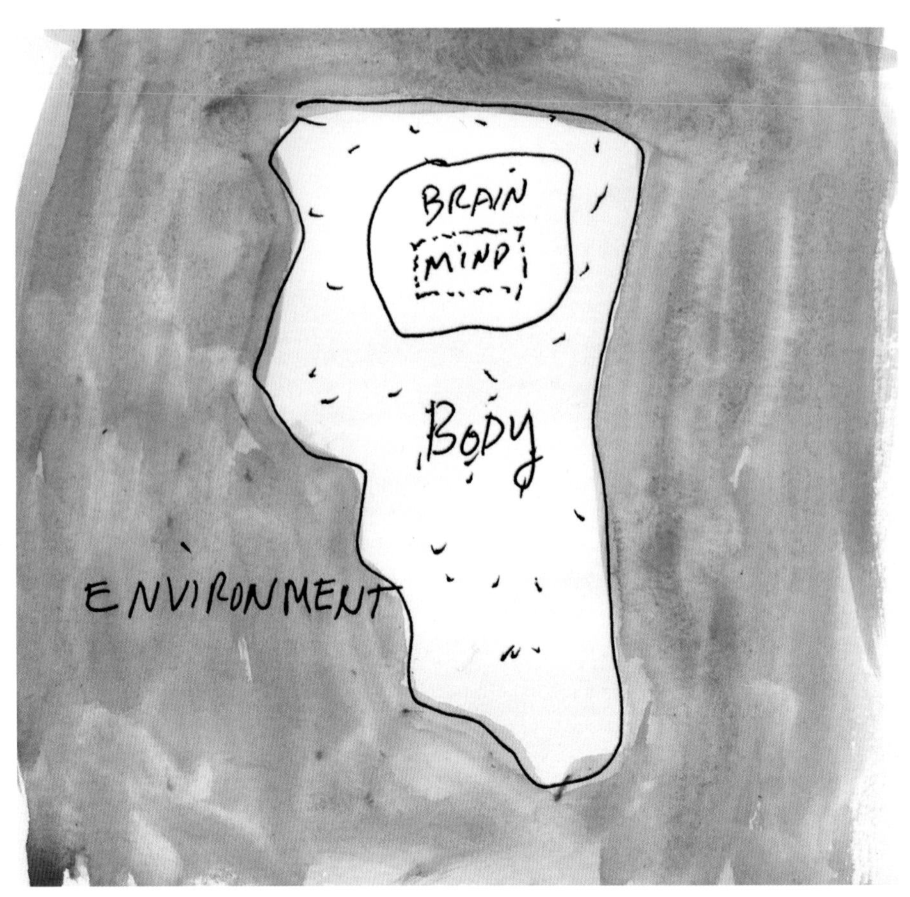

This diagram was made standing high on the island of Santorini, Greece, on September 16, 2016. The deep-cobalt-blue sea surrounds the island of white, sculptural-vernacular forms.

2. ENVIRONMENT / BODY / BRAIN / MIND

Each neuron in the human brain has an average of seven thousand synaptic connections to other neurons; think of the over one hundred billion neurons within the brain. The complexity is astonishing; when we reflect on the biological, physical, and environmental context, this complexity approaches the infinite.

In the diagram opposite, environment surrounds body. As you stand on an urban street corner, the city's buildings, materials, space, and light surround you. This surrounding architecture has a major effect on your inner layer of body, brain, and mind.

The environment surrounding the body deeply affects the body, which in turn affects the brain. The mind, however, is unpredictably intuitive. The mind works stochastically.

This stochastically driven mind embraces what is the soul and spirit of an individual—the poetic core of being. It is mysterious, not scientifically quantifiable.

When people die, their body weight remains the same as a few minutes before, when they were still alive. What departed? What is the soul of an individual? Weightless, stochastic spirit.

Dimitra Tsachrelia,
Eirini Tsachrelia,
Nicholas Karytinos,
SUSTAIN / ABILITY,
2016

3. STOCHASTIC / ANALOGICAL THINKING

Curiosity, imagination, and enthusiasm hold the power to ignite intuition. Aims coalesce and intuition flows as the joy of making art expands. The second law of thermodynamics states that all systems tend toward entropy. We counter this scientific fact with our creative acts.

The creative act, the opposite of entropy, puts energy back into our world. From outer space to inner space, shifting from a red spectrum, our Earth spins at one thousand miles per hour on the ecliptic tilt of 23.5 degrees. Finding new energy in the creative act is a cosmic connection.

The aleatoric thought process cannot be predetermined, unlike scientific and rational thought. Among the false boundaries separating architecture, sculpture, painting, and music, there exists a blurred zone of exciting potential. This fuzzy atmosphere promises the eminence of the new: the undetermined beginning, pregnant with imaginational force.

Creative architecture is connected in this way to all the arts—poetry, painting, sculpture, music, dance. They are all initiated in individual intuition, cross-discipline imagination, forms of stochastic and analogical thinking.

Analogical thinking in architecture has opened wide in the twenty-first century, now that we are finally free of dogmatic theories of rationalism, postmodernism, and deconstruction. Analogical thinking is an intertwining of architecture and all of the arts. Like an interconnected ecosystem, the arts and architecture are in symbiosis and can achieve new levels of correlation in the twenty-first century.

When we begin with an idea-analogue such as "a thing within a thing" or "a chiasma, an intertwining," we embed the formative architectural idea within the place as reciprocator. This initial interlinking can create a direct or inverse relationship. For example, linking by complementary contrast develops an inverse relationship. This idea may require another idea, such as "fusing architecture with landscape," to give it force. By analogy, we could say there is a mortised equivalence between landscape and architecture. Their correlation unfolds in the richly detailed development of the initial analogic thinking.

In an ambitious inverse ratio, one architecture can be the subtractive equivalent to another. For example, solid space could be echoed in reverse through void in an adjacent building. An inverse relationship on an urban scale, with metropolitan dimensions, correlates public space, architectural language, and an ecosystem in a new symbiosis.

Analogic thinking in its worldly embodiment at landscape and urban scales allows architectural thought to rise to the urgent metropolitan needs of our times. There is not sufficient precedent in the short history of New World architecture to provide relevant starting points for future times. Thoughtful architecture can begin with a new openness in stochastic and analogical thinking.

Creative tension at the outset of a project begins when embracing the real demands of a building program with the joy of the conceptual promiscuity of analogical thinking. We are curious; we search for a beginning; we imagine an idea that drives the design.

Twenty-first-century freedom in architecture allows us to begin from anything. The classical orders and the classical types are no longer a place of fertile beginning, nor is functionalism, nor the superficial styles of postmodernism or deconstruction.

The particular place—the climate, the cultural foundation and history of a place—provides a beginning that can build meaning into a site.

Meg Webster,
Cone of Water, 1987

Chapel of St. Ignatius,
Seattle University, 1997

Chapel Space	Color Field		Lens	
Processional Area	White		Clear	
Narthex	Red		Green	
Choir	Green		Red	
Nave East / West	Yellow	Blue	Blue	Yellow
Blessed Sacrament Chapel	Orange		Purple	
Reconciliation Chapel	Purple		Orange	
Bell Tower / Reflection Pool	Natural light		Water	

Complementary contrast colors in "seven bottles of light," posted on the website of the Chapel of St. Ignatius, Seattle University.

4. LIGHT: EXCITING NEURAL NETWORKS

Light is the main thing. Light is a natural phenomenon the complexity of which reveals the structure of human consciousness. Objects, including buildings, in their absorption and reflection of light, stimulate a human brain's neural networks,
in effect activating the brain. The more complex and nuanced the stimulation, the more fully the brain comes to life.
—LEBBEUS WOODS

Daily natural light is crucial to humans; research shows that circadian clocks within our bodies demand daylight. The "suprachiasmatic nucleus is the main director of our circadian clock," notes Alan Burdick in *Why Time Flies*. This cluster of twenty-thousand specialized neurons sits just above the optic chiasma—where the right and left nerves of the eyes cross. Even genes, which define who we are, function on a circadian schedule, regulated by sunlight.

The importance of natural light for physical and psychological well-being should now be recognized in all humanly inhabited environments. However, our current commercially driven building industry ignores health science and continues to produce thick, dark floor plans and to throw whole sections of urban territory into perennial shadow. Commercial forces aim for maximum real estate returns; the human aspects are ignored by obedient architects.

Up until the 1940s and the invention of air-conditioning, average metropolitan floor-plan depths were naturally constrained by the need to circulate light and air. Natural ventilation and light will penetrate into a building up to about 30 feet (9 meters) from the perimeter wall, which would set the thickness of a plan at a maximum of 60 feet (18 meters). Thus were created great works such as Raymond Hood's Rockefeller Center.

Today, the light and air dimension is often ignored by architects and developers. From the 1970s to today, the absence of natural light due to thick, poorly proportioned floor plans and sections presents a psychological and health problem. Scientific evidence for the urgency of change now exists.

During the eighteenth and nineteenth centuries, the nighttime environment of cities changed only slightly. The twentieth century, however, brought the sudden shock of vast quantities of night light, which alters our perception of the shape and form of urban space.

New York City's Times Square is a dirty, gray, crowded intersection by day, but at night it is an astonishing volume of glowing light—a space defined by light, color, and atmospheric conditions. When there is a

The Pantheon, Rome, ca. 113–125 CE

slight mist or haze in Manhattan's air at night, Times Square is a space of liquid color, and a shaft of light forms over skyscrapers farther south, such as the Empire State Building and the Woolworth Building.

The power and importance of natural light is a central aspect of Greek thought and philosophy. When the philosopher Diogenes was asked by Alexander the Great what in the whole of this world he wanted, Diogenes asked the emperor to get out of his sunlight. In the tenth century BCE, the steep hillside of Delphi was designated the sanctuary of Apollo, the Greek god of light. Later, in the eighth century BCE, Delphi became the site of the Oracle, who foretold the future to the ancient people of the Mediterranean.

In ancient Chinese philosophy, light is a major aspect of the fundamental concept of yin and yang. Yang is the masculine—white, light, south, the sun—while yin is the feminine—darkness, water, north, the moon.

A most poetic ancient architectural embodiment of light is the Pantheon in Rome. As a student, I lived behind the Pantheon and went into it every morning (before the tourists) to experience how different the light was every day. The great oculus in the orb's summit always casts a slightly different light.

The revolutions in science we experience today often are the product of light and its speed: fiber-optic transmission, for example. Even our future computers may run on light.

Transmitting the force and spiritual power of daylight has been a core aim of our architecture for forty years. The perceptual spirit and metaphysical strength of architecture are driven by the quality of light and shadow shaped by solids and voids, by opacities and transparencies and translucencies. What the eyes see and the senses feel in relation to architecture is formed according to conditions of light and shadow. Natural light, with its ethereal variety of changes, fundamentally orchestrates the intensities of architecture and cities.

Space T2, Rhinebeck,
New York, 2016

Museum of
Contemporary Art
Kiasma, Helsinki,
Finland, 1993–98

Knut Hamsun Center,
Hamarøy, Norway,
1994–2009

The Holl House in Manchester, Washington, at Puget Sound, was designed for my parents in 1974 and shown here in June 2019. The house is two squares in plan with 1:1.618 proportions guiding all decisions. Forty-four years later, the design is still fresh.

5. LAKE OF THE MIND: WATER AND LIGHT

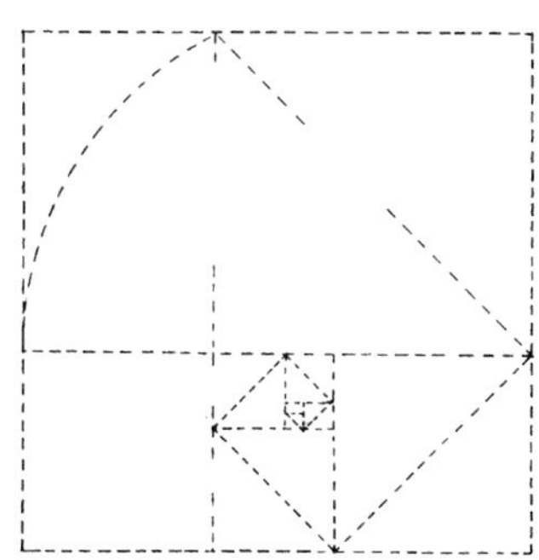

The lake is a large tranquil eye.
—GASTON BACHELARD, *Water and Dreams*

The field of neuroscience has recently unveiled the brain's method of interpreting spatial and other information. "Points in space map to arrangements of retinal neurons somewhat in the way that musical notes map to keys on a piano," Alan Burdick writes in *Why Time Flies*.

There is a millisecond time lag before a given stimulus reaches the brain. Some signals fire, while others slightly lag. This phenomenon is illustrated "by picturing the brain as the surface of a lake," writes the American psychologist Karl Lashley. Ripples of impulse crisscross the brain as if in water.

Water and light have been essential to me since my childhood overlooking the expanse of Puget Sound between Seattle and Manchester, Washington. The rising sun glances off the tops of the water in sparkling glints of light, changing every day. The low winter sun is supercharged by its reflection in water, multiplying the effects of light. Even the rise of the moon leaves a magical track of light stretching across the water to the horizon.

Our bodies are more than half water, and 71 percent of the Earth's surface is covered by water, so it is not surprising that the psychological and health benefits of natural light are multiplied by proximity to water. We continue to explore this essential experience, captured by the fusion of architecture and landscape in a rich variety of examples.

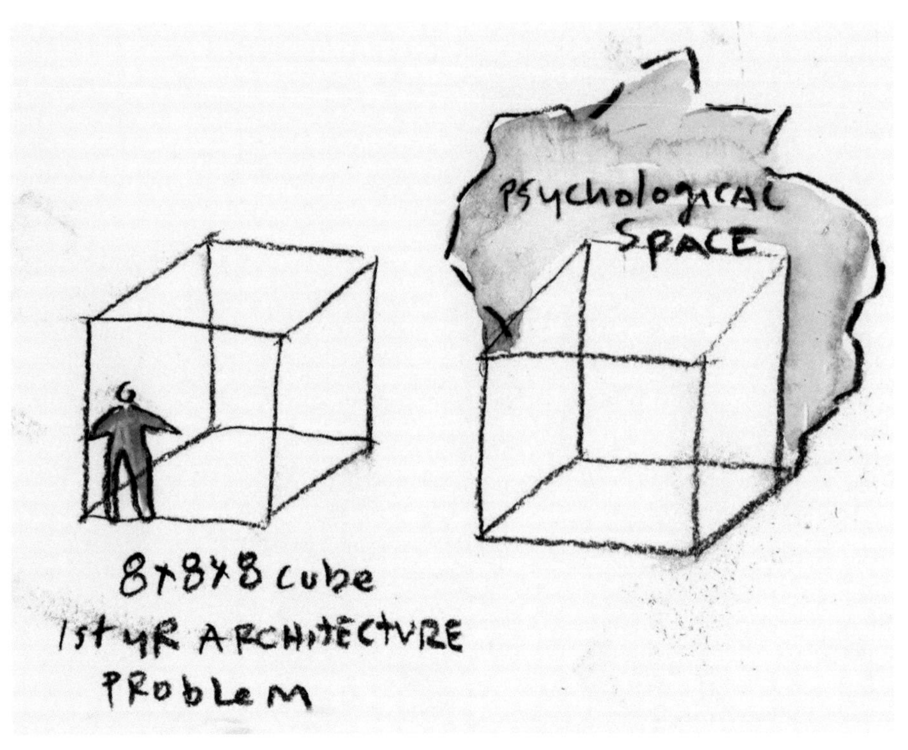

Cold Jacket, 2016
T2 Reserve:
a space formed by
laminated glass tubes
in light.

6. PSYCHOLOGICAL SPACE

As first-year students at the University of Washington in 1967, we were asked to design an 8-foot (2.4-meter) cube of space to serve all aspects of daily existence: living, working, eating, sleeping. I drew a cube with a dotted line to a curvilinear shape indicating psychological space; I argued that the curved space was a necessary extension of the functional cube. My professors, a mix of functionalists and regionalists, reluctantly accepted this early project.

In 2009 I wrote *Urbanisms: Working with Doubt*, which argues for the psychological and poetic in the creation of urban plans. The fusing of landscape, urbanism, and architecture has become a new ground for exploration. As our interiors are often conceived as exteriors, so the relation of building to grounds might be reversed or integrated. Architecture demands to be integrated with landscape and urbanism, rooted in deep connections to site, culture, and climate rather than an applied signature style. Working with openness and doubt at the outset of each project can yield works engaging both site and culture.

Yet our present profession of architecture, where one firm is hired for the shell and core, another for interiors, and still others for landscape and marketing, has sold its psychological potential to the whims of market economy. Resistance to this disconnection is essential for the psychological health of our urban futures—quality before quantity.

On a macro scale, mental space expands to the psychological field of urban space. The simultaneous interactions of topography, program, lines of urban movement, materials, and light come together to manifest the spirit of an urban place. The psychological effects of sound must be considered, as well as other temporal fragmentations. In this regard, architecture produces desire. The exhilaration we find when we walk into the space between or inside certain buildings produces a kind of psychological space. It can represent an experience we never had before and want to repeat. The recognition of spatial and material phenomena meets the imagination. The power of changing light and the spatial energy of the route of movement fuse together into something totally new to us, a new desire. This is a core aspect of psychological space.

An installation sculpture by Ai Weiwei, designed for 'T' Space, 2013. Created in 2010, our not-for-profit foundation aims to sustain the arts. To date, we have had more than twenty-two exhibitions—each with poetry, music, and dance.

7. NEGATIVE CAPABILITY

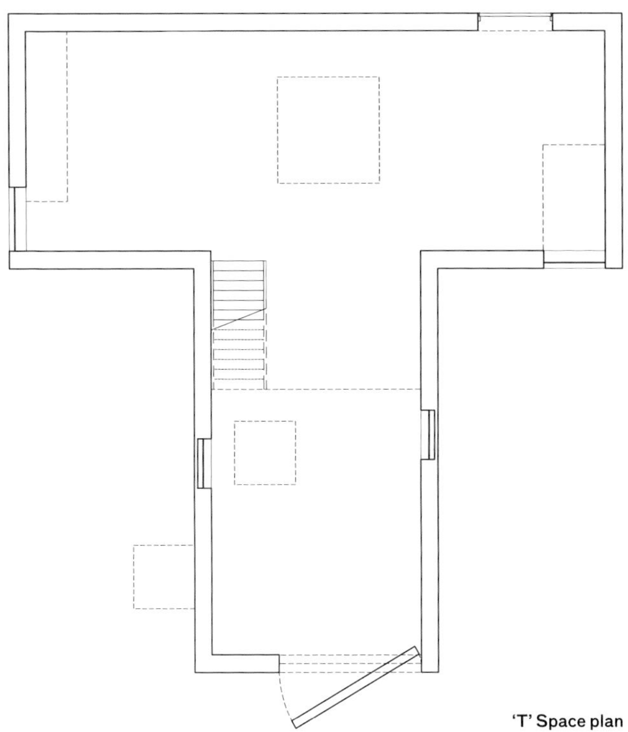

'T' Space plan

How, in the world we inhabit today, can we think of the way forward as artists and architects? Given income inequality in the extreme, pollution and looming climate change, the prevalence of fake news, incompetent, lying leaders, and the architectural excess of the one percent, where is architecture's capability?

John Keats used the term *negative capability* in 1817: "When a man is capable of being in uncertainties, mysteries, doubts, without any irritable reaching after fact and reason" yet can pursue artistic beauty. As we don't have answers today, we could ask relevant questions; we might employ a twenty-first-century version of this negative capability. This is, briefly, to take in all the negative aspects of the civilization around us and to gather them inside oneself—within the spirit—and still make a creative contribution.

As the poet Kenneth Rexroth said, "Against the ruin of the world, there is only one defense—the creative act."

tspacerhinebeck.org
vimeo.com/228857467

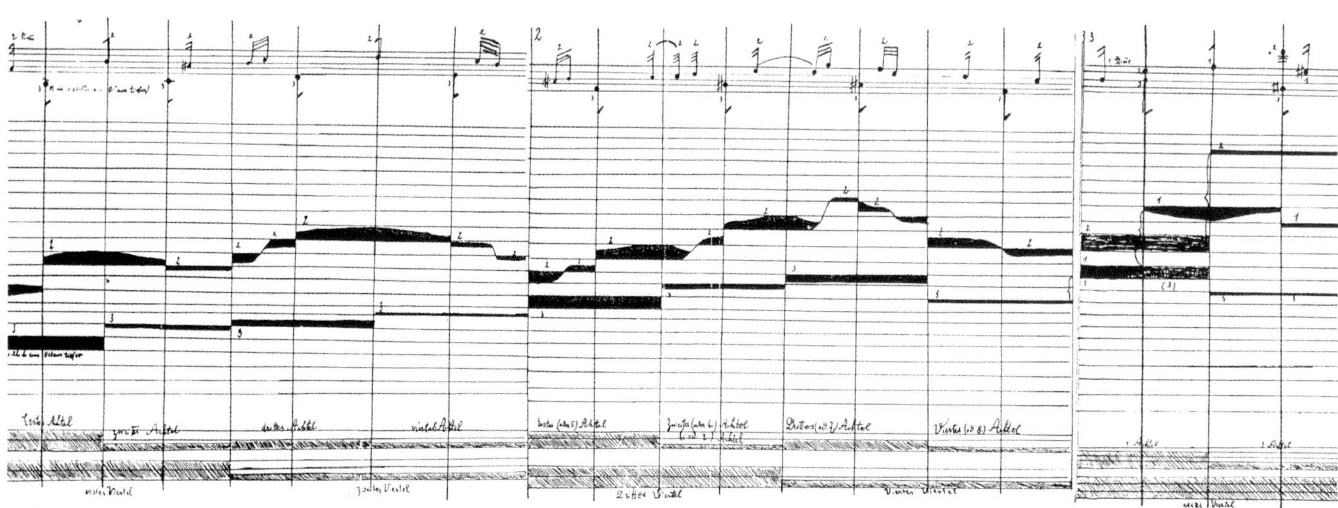

top
Stretto House, Dallas, Texas, 1989
AIA Dallas 25-Year Award, Residential, 2018

above
Paul Klee, drawing from sketchbook

8. ARCHITECTONICS OF MUSIC

Music... is the 'arithmetic of sound' just as optics is 'the geometry of light.'
—CLAUDE DEBUSSY

Neuroscientist Oliver Sacks argues in *Musicophilia* for the unique capabilities of music. In amazing case studies, he reveals how the wordless phenomenon of music activates the brain. Likewise, architecture activates the brain.

The Architectonics of Music is a graduate design studio we have taught for over ten years at the Graduate School of Architecture, Planning and Preservation at Columbia University. Music, like architecture, is an immersive experience; it surrounds you. You can turn away from a painting or a sculpture, while music and architecture engulf the body in space.

Music is the interpenetration of space and sound across time. Space and light are at the core of architecture, while sound and time are at the elemental core of music.

Both of these art disciplines revolve around materiality. Where music has a materiality in instrumentation and sound, architecture has an analogue in light and space. We can draw the following equation:

$$\frac{\text{Material} \times \text{Sound}}{\text{TIME}} = \frac{\text{Material} \times \text{Light}}{\text{SPACE}}$$

An example of music's materiality is a 1936 composition by Béla Bartók, *Music for Strings, Percussion and Celesta*. This piece in four movements has a distinct division between heavy (percussion) and light (strings); Bartók located the string section across the stage from the percussion section to emphasize the heavy and light. In 1989 we built the Stretto House in Dallas, Texas, based precisely on this idea in Bartók's composition. Bartók also composed using the golden section proportion of 1:1.618. The golden section is the simplest, most ancient tool for the organization of pleasing proportion, both in sound and space.

Concept sketch for Rubenstein Commons, Institute for Advanced Study, 2016

9. SOCIAL CONDENSERS

At a time of increasing privatization of urban space, we work toward an architecture of public spaces, social offerings, and inspiring spatial energy.

The term *social condenser* was coined by Moisei Ginzburg, the architect of the now-ruined Narkomfin Building, Moscow, 1932.

To invigorate the term, we use it in the context of our aim of socially activating interior or exterior public spaces.

Architecture has the potential to change the way we live our daily lives; architecture can provide public spaces that have an influence on behavior.

Our projects are envisioned partly as providing spaces that act as social condensers in various ways.

For example, the Hunters Point Community Library is more than a place of books and study. It is a space that invites all new immigrants in the borough of Queens to receive assistance with language and applications, while it also provides a forum for community meetings, special lectures, readings, and events.

The Lewis Arts Complex forms a new entrance for the Princeton University campus while introducing the public to the variety of performing arts activities within. Below the public space of the new quad, between three buildings, we realized a large forum where students from all disciplines can meet and interact.

Fundamental Aims

—

1. To provide public spaces open to all (not the one percent versus the ninety-nine percent)
2. To give spatial energy to this openness via a sense of invitation and urban porosity
3. To excite potential creativity and interaction via architecture
4. To carry this interactive energy beyond the boundary of the site to the campus and the public streets
5. To apply the most advanced science and technology to establish an environmental example for the future

MAKING

2005
2007
2008
2009
2010
2011
2012
2013
2014
2015
2016
2017
2018

Projects in bold have been built or are under construction.

HERNING MUSEUM OF CONTEMPORARY ART

Herning, Denmark
2005–9
Competition: First Place

As a fusion of landscape and architecture, the Herning Museum of Contemporary Art builds its site. Transforming a flat field, a new landscape of grass mounds and pools conceals parking and service areas while shaping inspiring bermed landscape spaces focused on reflecting pools oriented toward the southern sun.

The curved roof sections of the museum align with this built site. All gallery spaces are orthogonal and simple with fine proportions in respect to the art, while overhead the curved roof sections bring in natural light. The internal gallery walls can be moved per curators' requirements.

The arte povera artist Piero Manzoni made many of his most important works in a shirt factory next to this site—thus, our concept of shirt sleeves draped over gallery boxes (see the early concept sketch above).

A fabric theme is continued in the fabric-formed texture of the white concrete walls of the elevations. A geothermal HVAC system and gray-water recycling are among several green features that establish this museum as exemplary twenty-first-century architecture.

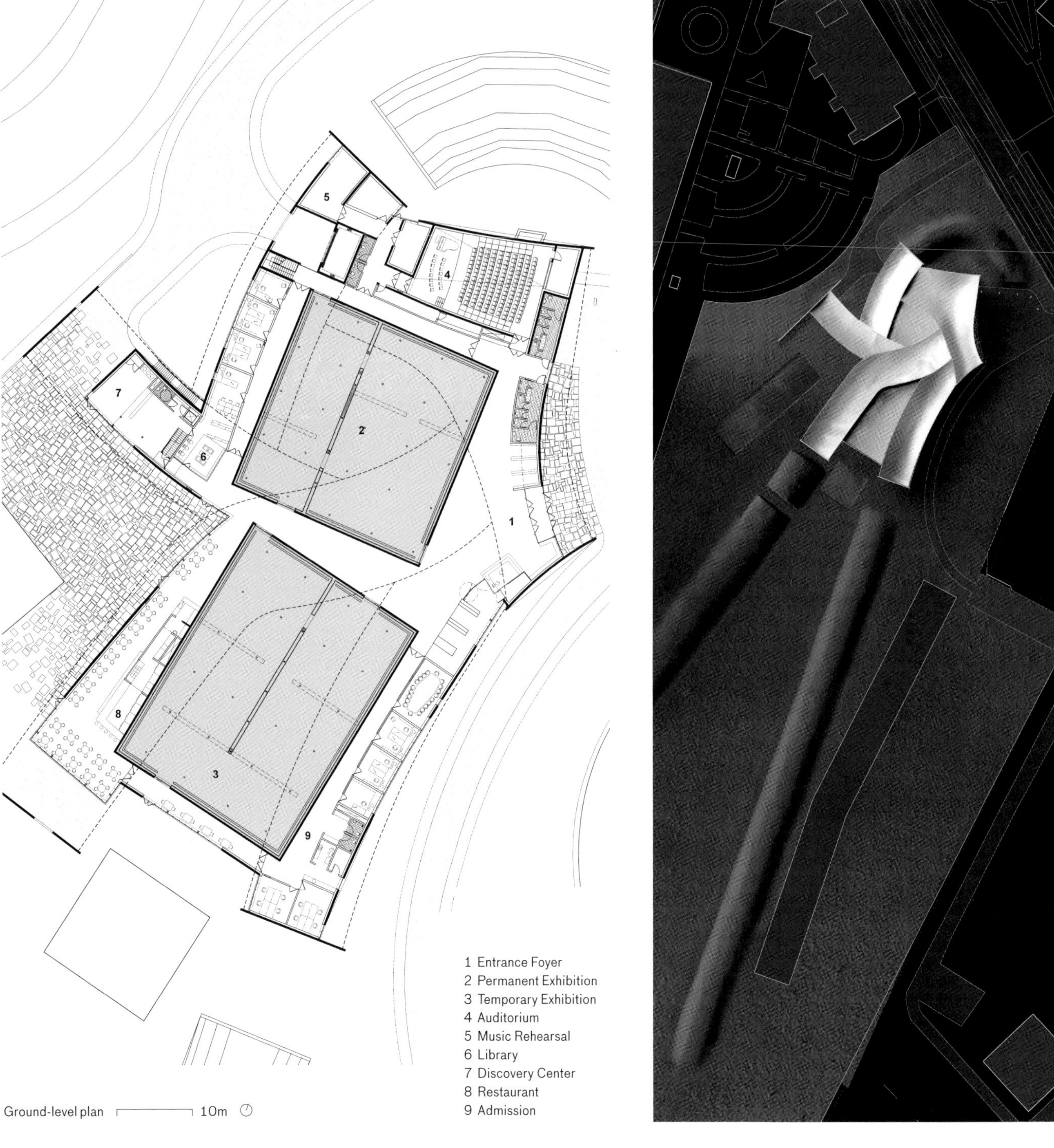

Ground-level plan 10m

1 Entrance Foyer
2 Permanent Exhibition
3 Temporary Exhibition
4 Auditorium
5 Music Rehearsal
6 Library
7 Discovery Center
8 Restaurant
9 Admission

CITÉ DE L'OCÉAN ET DU SURF

Biarritz, France
2005–11
Competition: First Place

The Cité de l'Océan et du Surf museum raises awareness of oceanic issues and explores educational and scientific aspects of the surf and sea and their role in our leisure, science, and ecology.

The building form derives from the spatial concept "under the sky / under the sea." We shaped the building with the idea of a central gathering plaza open to the sky and to the sea horizon in the distance. This *place de l'océan*, with its curved, under-the-sky shape, determines the character of the main exhibition space, the under-the-sea shape.

The building's spatial qualities are first experienced in the entrance, where ramps pass along the dynamic curved surface and exhibition projections animate and change the light.

The western edges of the site are slightly cupped, connecting the forms with landscape on axis to the ocean and concealing flanking parked cars.

The master plan connects the new museum to the oceanfront. The principle of organization of the section is broken by two glass "boulders," which contain a restaurant and surfers' kiosk. This activates the central outdoor space and projects analogically to two great boulders in the distance on the Biarritz beach.

The roof lilts toward the horizon and contains a skate pool and an open porch that connects to a game area. Built in white titanium concrete, the roof plaza is made of hand-set Portuguese stones.

Master plan connecting glass boulders with great boulders on the Biarritz beach

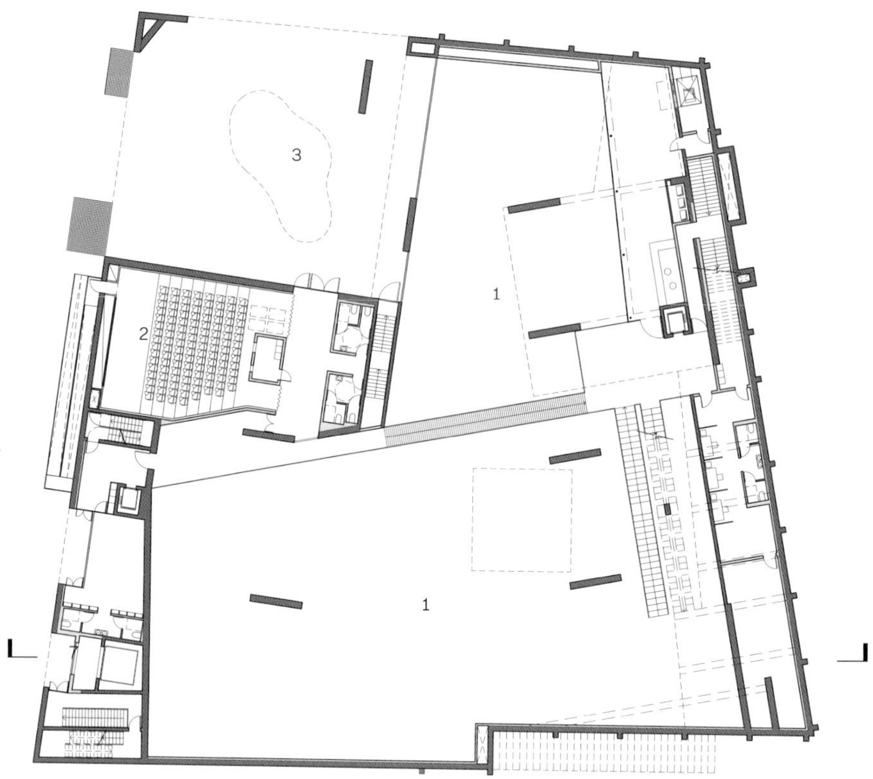

Pavilion-level plan 10m

1 Exhibition
2 Auditorium
3 Pool Above
4 Rooftop Terrace
5 Surfers' Kiosk
6 Restaurant
7 Loading Dock
8 Entrance Reception

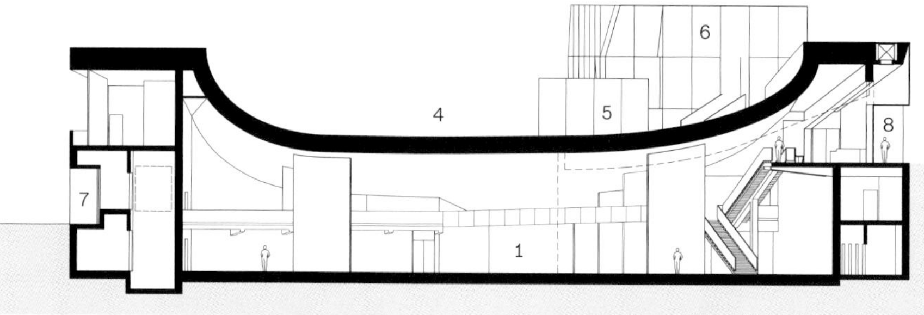

Section 10m

Glowing light in the base of the pool rises from the Forum below.

LEWIS ARTS COMPLEX
PRINCETON UNIVERSITY

Princeton, New Jersey, USA
2007–17

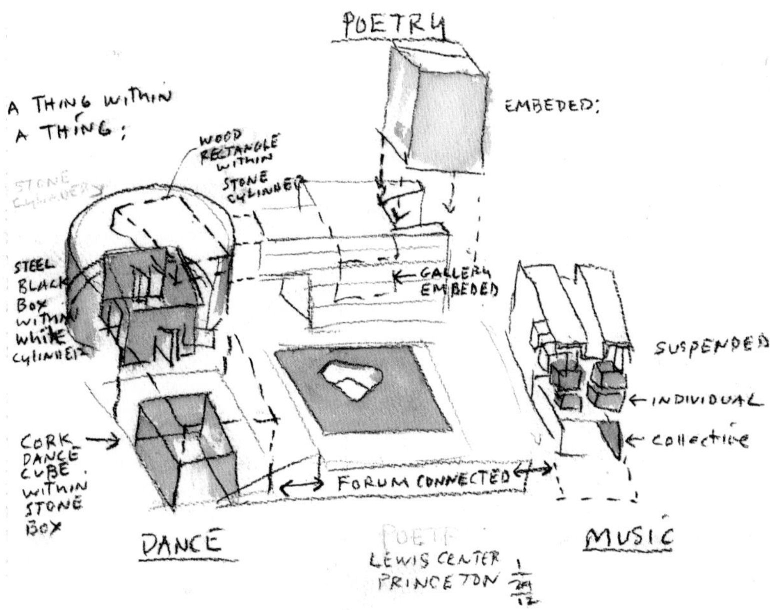

The story of this project began when the president of Princeton University, Shirley M. Tilghman, launched an initiative to give new prominence to the arts on the Princeton campus. Her idea of this project as a campus gateway presenting the arts was a radical concept.

On December 8, 2007, we presented against several other teams, including David Chipperfield (an earlier scheme for the Lewis Arts Complex by Renzo Piano had previously been rejected).

We showed a small, white model, proposing a center made of three buildings forming a quadrangle, with a reflecting pool lighting a big, collective space that we called the Forum.

Even though this large space was not in Princeton's program, the visionary Tilghman chose us to be the architect. As the site was partially in Princeton township and partially on the university campus, many complicated political presentations of the project stretched its development out over ten years, until it opened on October 7, 2017.

The Lewis Arts Complex includes a theater and dance building, an arts building, and a music building with instrumental rehearsal and practice rooms. All three buildings are integrated in the below-ground Forum.

The project aims to create a new campus gateway, shaping campus space while maximizing porosity. Views overlooking the dance and theater practice spaces and the orchestral rehearsal space are aimed at provoking curiosity and interaction.

vimeo.com/288356972

above
Concept sketch shows the three buildings shaping a quadrangle, with a pool providing light to the social-condenser Forum.

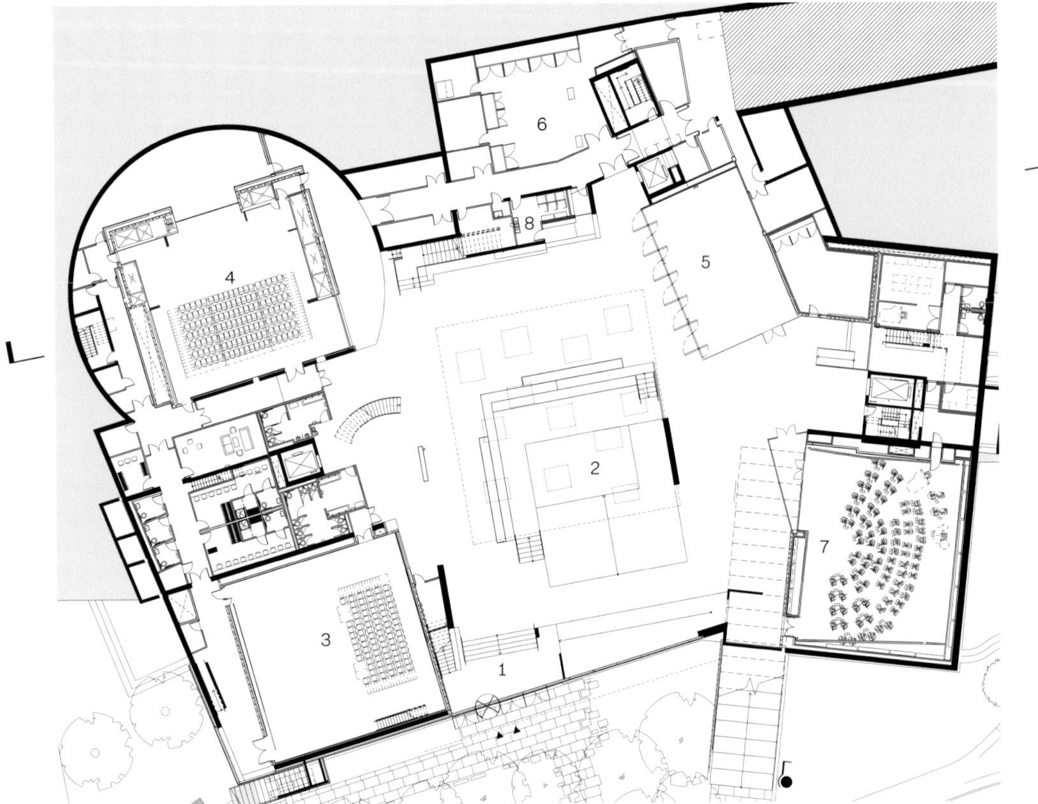

Lower-level plan 50'

1 Entry
2 Forum
3 Dance Theater
4 Black Box Theater
5 Colab
6 Shop
7 Instrumental Rehearsal
8 Coffee / Concession
9 Acting Studio
10 Administration

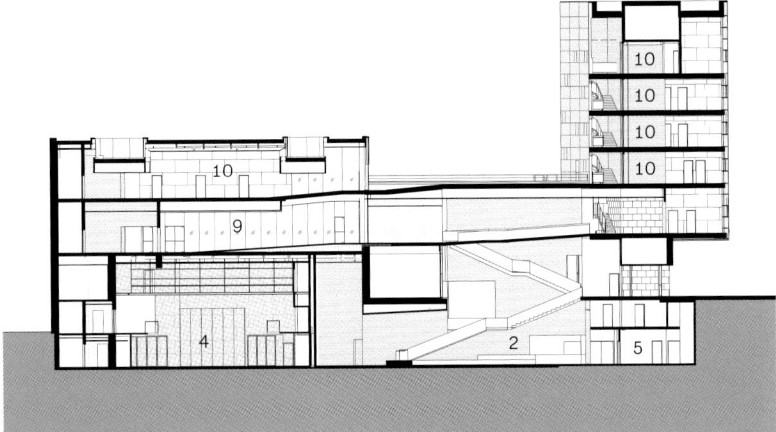

Section 50'

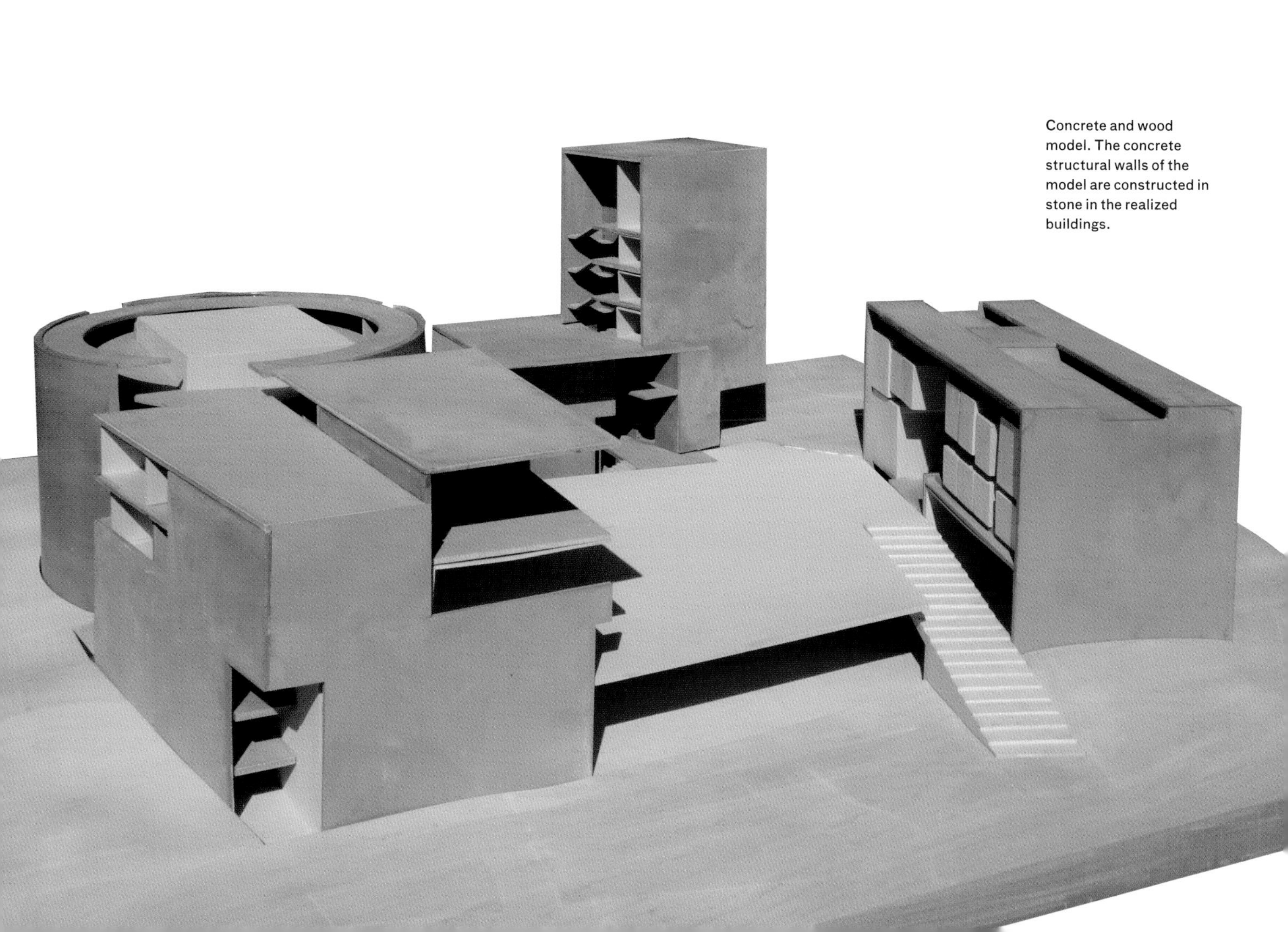

Concrete and wood model. The concrete structural walls of the model are constructed in stone in the realized buildings.

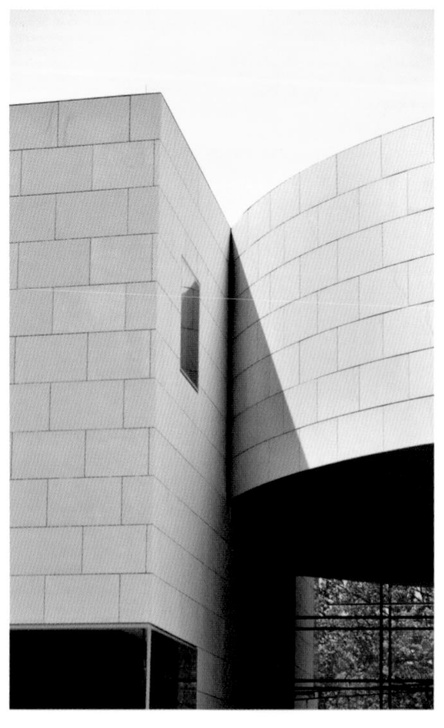

top left
Two-million-year-old Lecce stone from a quarry opened two thousand years ago by Romans in Lecce, Italy: a projection of the distant past into the future

top middle
The Dancing Stair with labanotation perforation

top right
Custom door handle

left
Embossed concrete shows the campus plan.

Collective

Individual practice rooms in wood are suspended on steel rods over the collective orchestral practice hall. Concrete support beams run in the long direction.

CAMPBELL SPORTS CENTER
COLUMBIA UNIVERSITY

New York, New York, USA
2008–13

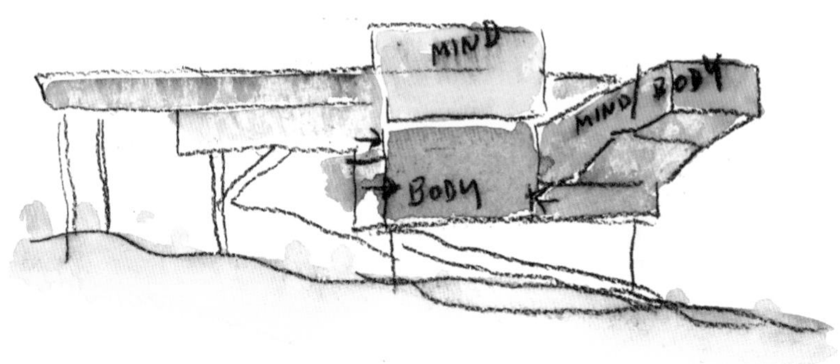

Located on the corner of West 218th Street and Broadway—at the northernmost edge of Manhattan, where Broadway crosses Tenth Avenue and the elevated tracks of the 1 subway line—the Campbell Sports Center forms a new gateway to the Baker Athletics Complex, the primary site for Columbia University's outdoor sports program.

The facility, which adds approximately 48,000 square feet (4,459 square meters) of space to the complex, houses strength and conditioning spaces, offices for varsity sports, theater-style meeting rooms, a hospitality suite, and student-athlete study rooms.

The Campbell Sports Center serves the mind, the body, and the mind/body of aspiring scholar-athletes. The design concept, "points on the ground, lines in space" (inspired by field-play diagrams used for football, soccer, and baseball), was developed from point foundations on the sloping site. Just as points and lines in diagrams yield physical push and pull on the field, the building's elevations push and pull in space.

The building shapes the street corner, then lifts up to form a portal connecting the urban streetscape and the playing field. Extending over a stepped landscape, blue soffits heighten the openness of the urban-scale portico. Terraces and external stairs, which serve as lines in space, draw the field play onto and into the building; their upper levels provide views over the field and Manhattan.

Presentation video: vimeo.com/70431939

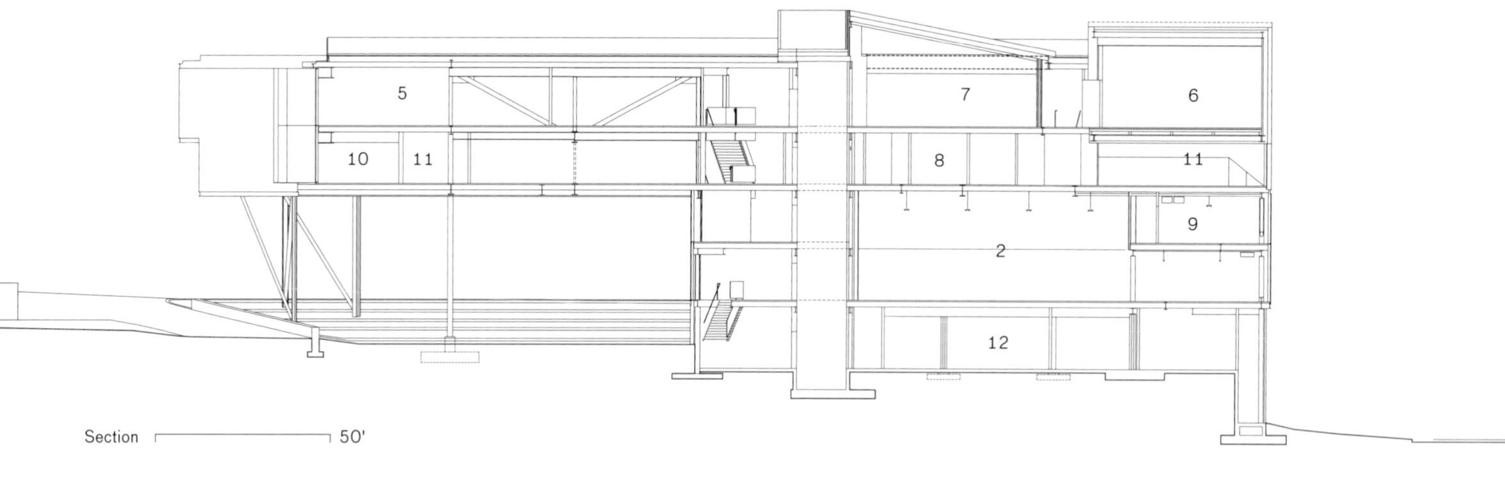

Section 50'

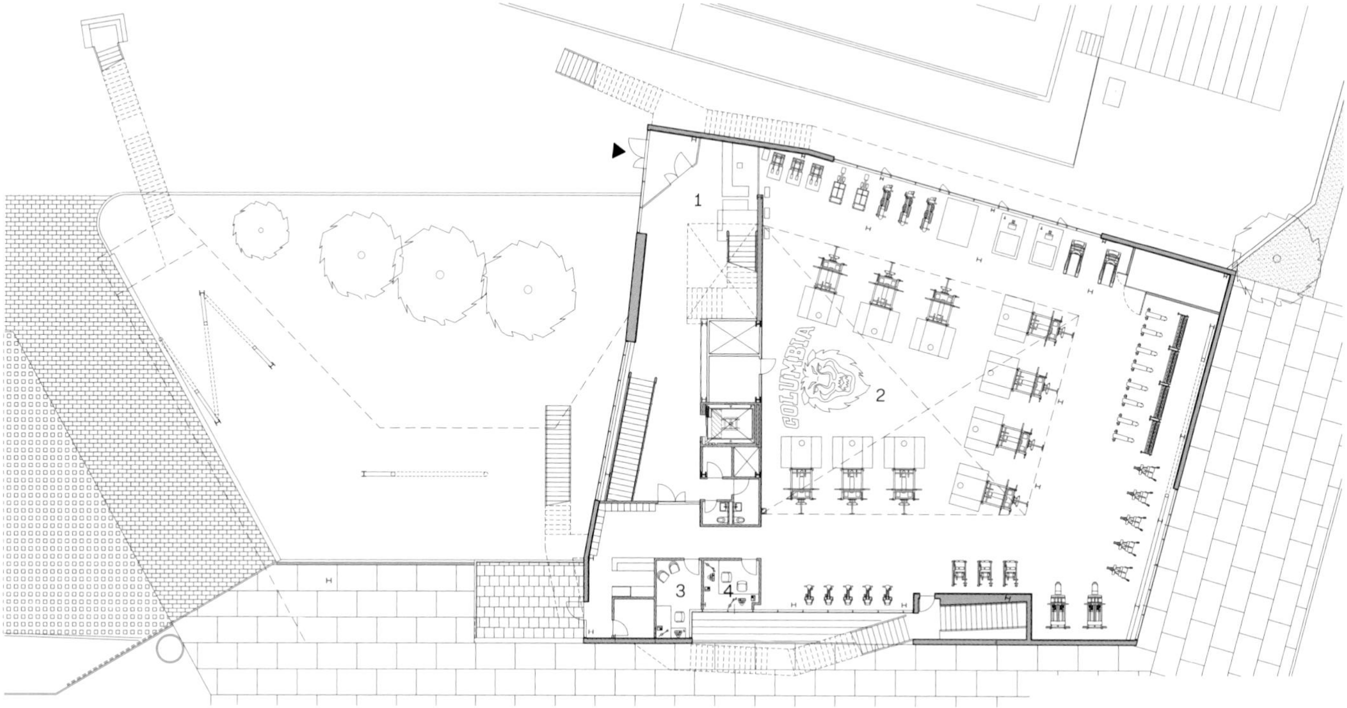

Open portico and second level 50'

1 Main Entrance and Lobby
2 Strength and Conditioning
3 Head Coach's Office
4 Assistant Coach's Office
5 Student Athlete Study Center
6 Student Athlete Meeting Room
7 Hospitality Suite
8 Locker Room
9 Conference Room
10 Office
11 Meeting Room
12 Service Space

Lines in space of exit stair

L Tower and M Tower with bridges touching each other over the harbor

LM HARBOUR GATEWAY

Copenhagen, Denmark
2008–
Competition: First Place

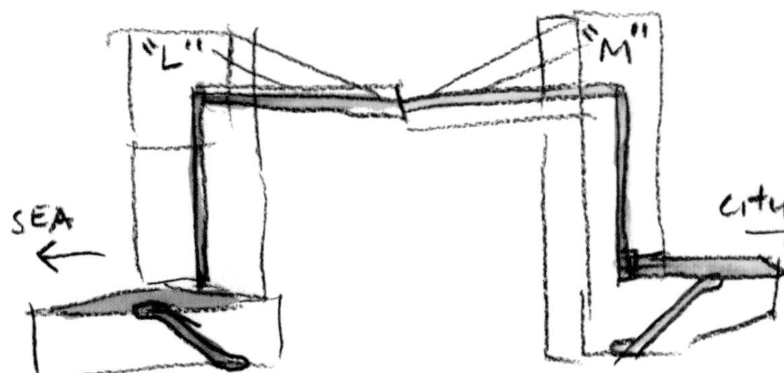

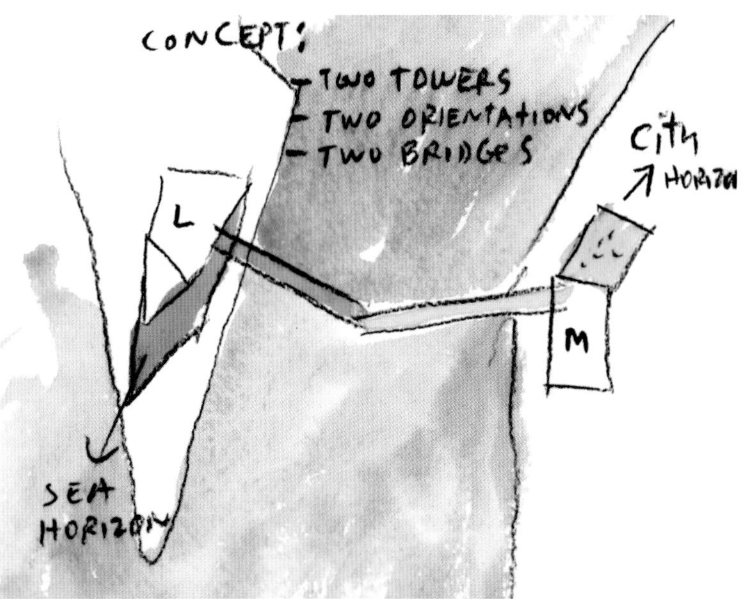

The international competition for this harbor gate required a pedestrian bridge connection high enough for cruise ships to pass under. This 558-foot (170 meter) span, 223 feet high (68 meters), will be achieved with two cable-stayed bridges, which join like a handshake over the harbor. The M Tower is a hybrid program of hotel, offices, and cafés, which will achieve German Sustainable Building Council Gold status, in recognition of its geothermal heating and cooling and a solar array. Because of the economic collapse of 2008, the project was put on hold. It was restarted in 2018; construction drawings are in progress at the time of this writing.

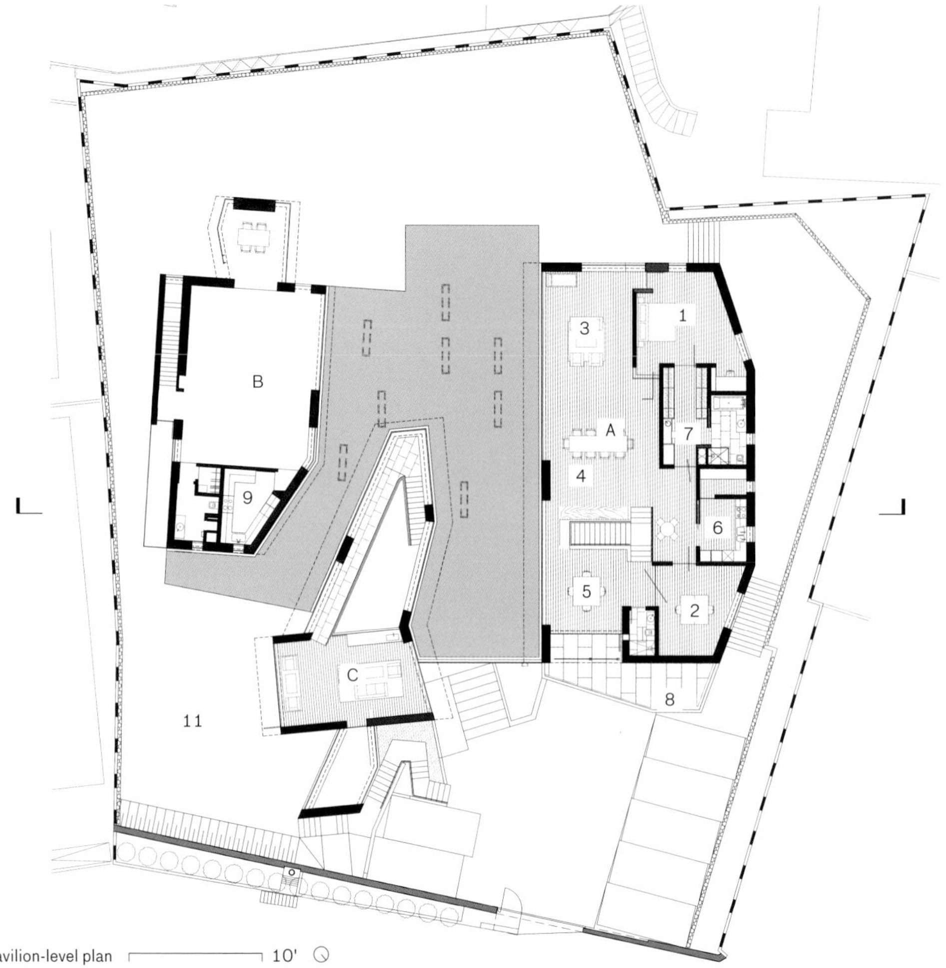

Pavilion-level plan 10'

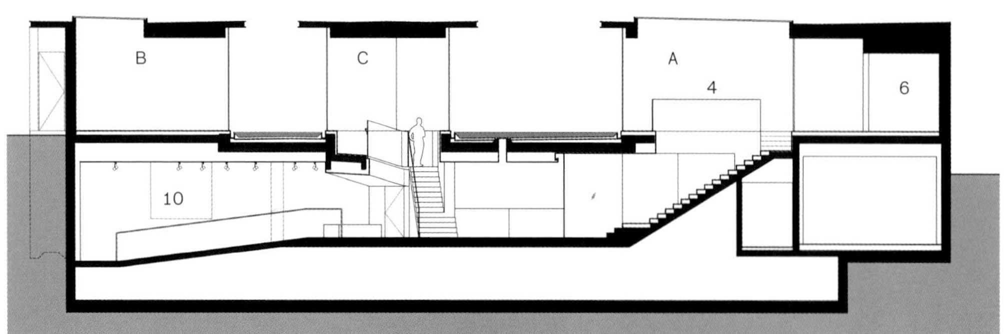

Section 10'

A Residence
B Event Space
C Reception

1 Master Bedroom
2 Library / Bedroom
3 Living
4 Dining
5 Meeting Room
6 Kitchen
7 Dressing Room
8 Terrace
9 Service Kitchen
10 Gallery
11 Garden

DAEYANG GALLERY AND HOUSE

Seoul, South Korea
2008–12

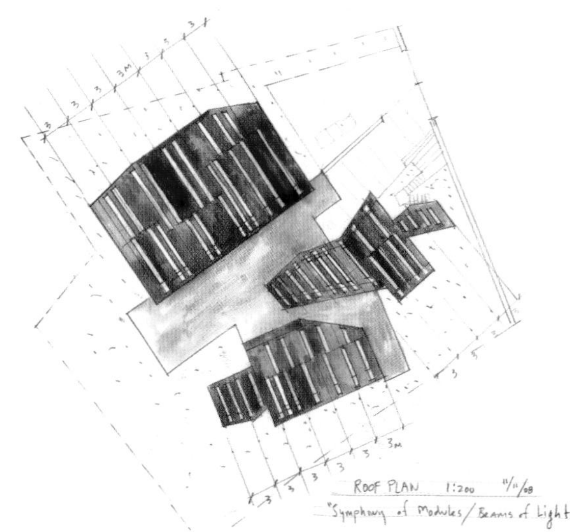

The man who dies thus rich dies disgraced.
—ANDREW CARNEGIE, 1889

The owner of Daeyang Shipping Co. in South Korea requested a design for a gallery and house in the Gangbuk district of Seoul. We based the house on the 1967 musical score *Symphony of Modules* by the composer István Anhalt.

A sheet of water over the gallery joins three pavilions: an entrance, a residence, and an event space.

As in the sketch for the score, there are fifty-five skylights in the patina copper pavilions. The project is geothermally heated and cooled. The pool, designed to freeze in winter, allows light into the gallery through thin ice.

Later, the client, You Keun Chung, formed the Miracle for Africa Foundation, sold his shipping company, and dedicated himself to building hospitals and a new campus for Malawi.

This project led directly to our project for the Malawi Library and campus plan in Lilongwe, Malawi (see page 138).

Presentation video: vimeo.com/45443501

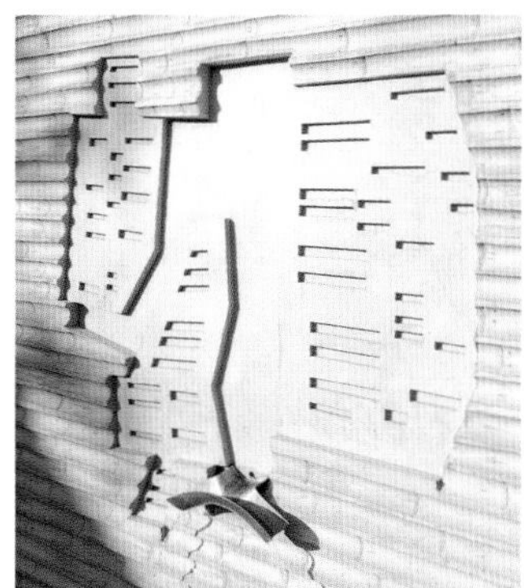

SA187
Diversion
End
20

REID BUILDING
GLASGOW SCHOOL OF ART

Glasgow, Scotland, United Kingdom
2009–14
Competition: First Place

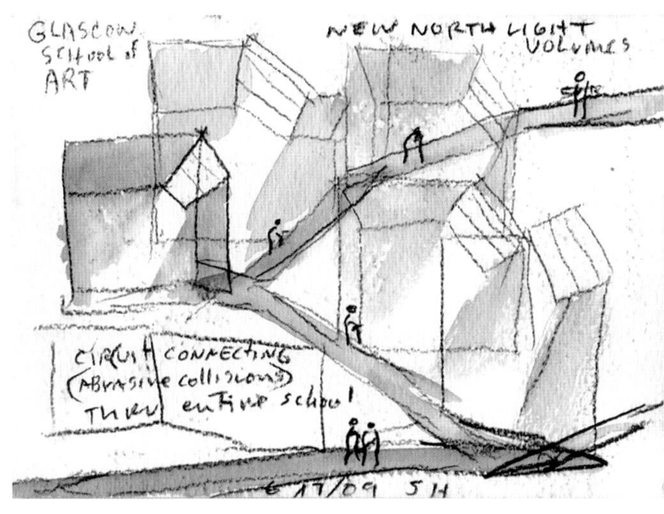

This project began with a competition. More than one hundred entries were narrowed to six finalists for a 121,094-square-foot (11,250-square-meter) addition to the historic monument of Charles Rennie Mackintosh's 1909 Glasgow School of Art.

While the original has a thick stone skin and thin bones, the new building has thick concrete bones and a thin skin. The translucent materiality is considered in complementary contrast to the masonry of the Mackintosh building—volumes of light express the school's activity in the urban fabric.

The concept of "driven voids of light" integrates structure, HVAC, spatial modulation, and light. The driven-void light shafts deliver natural light throughout the building.

A circuit of connection through the Reid Building encourages creative abrasion across and among departments that is central to the workings of the school. The open circuit of stepped ramps links all major spaces—lobby, exhibition space, project spaces, lecture theater, seminar rooms, studios, workshops, and green terraces—for informal gatherings and exhibitions.

Unbelievably, in June 2018, the Mackintosh building tragically burned for a second time in four years. We are joining all fundraising efforts to rebuild Mackintosh's masterpiece.

Presentation video: vimeo.com/101410201
Fundraising video: vimeo.com/65395492

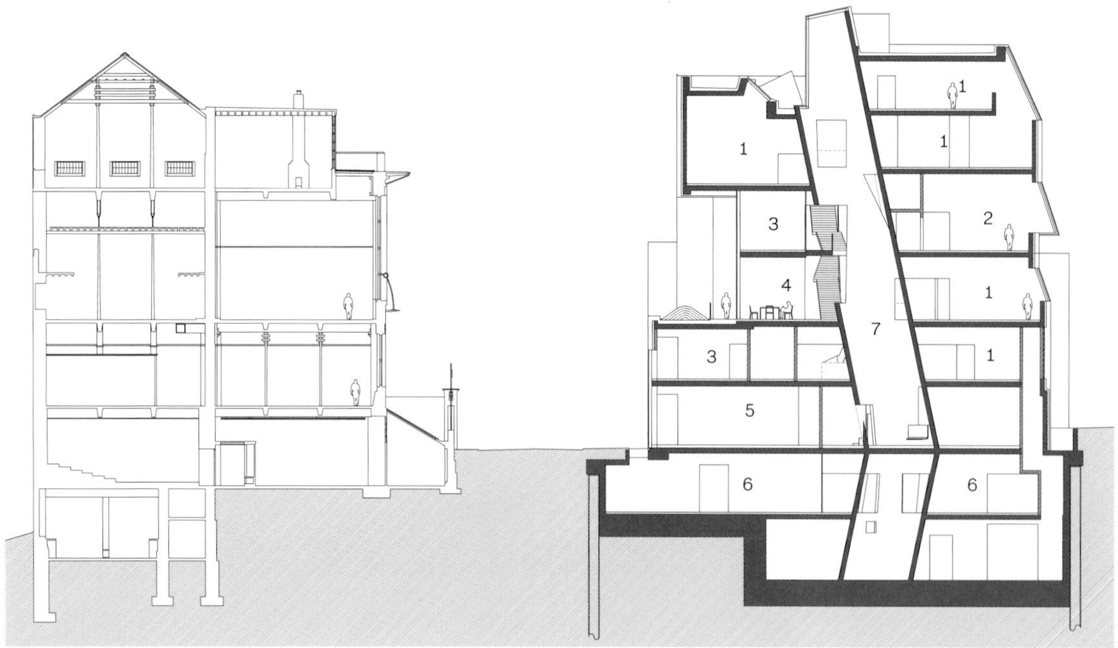

Section, 1909, Mackintosh 10m

Section, 2014 10m

1 Studio
2 Lab
3 Office
4 Refectory
5 Exhibition Space
6 Workshop Space
7 Driven Void of Light

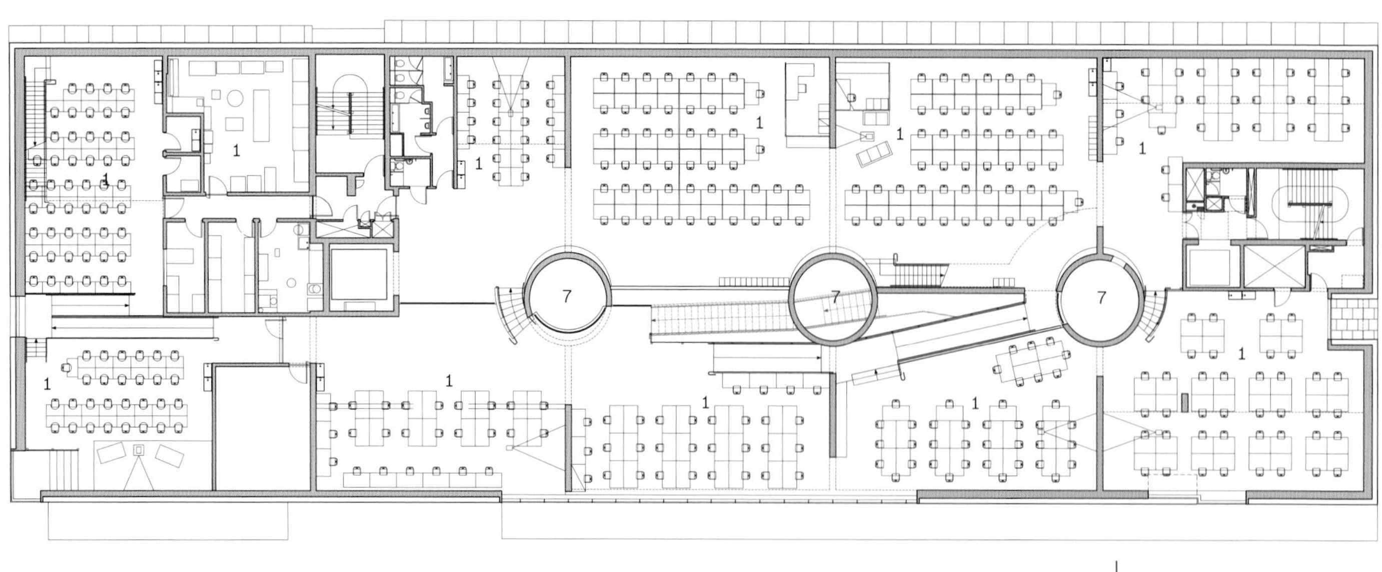

Fourth-floor plan 10m

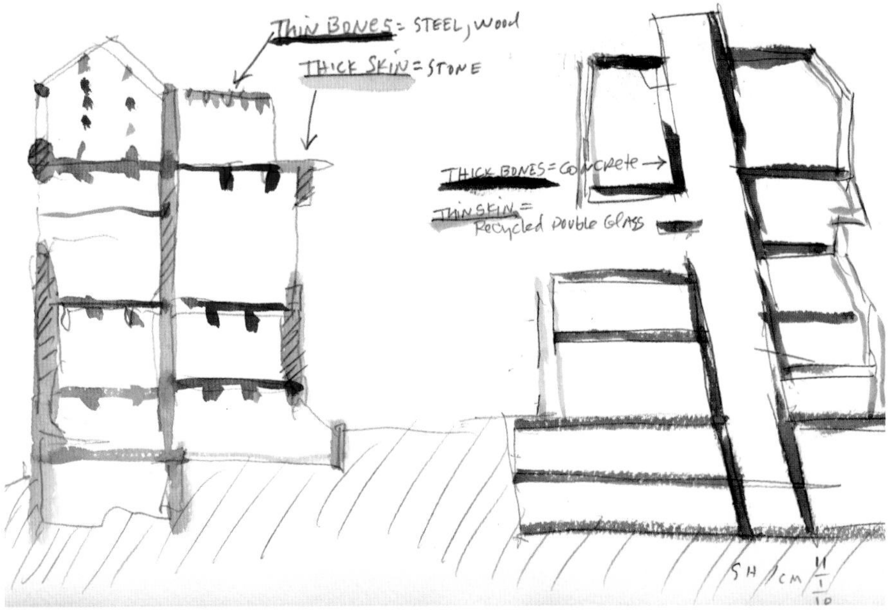

top
Driven voids of light bring in sunshine and fresh air, provide structural support, and create space for potential creative use.

right
Concept sketch, 2010

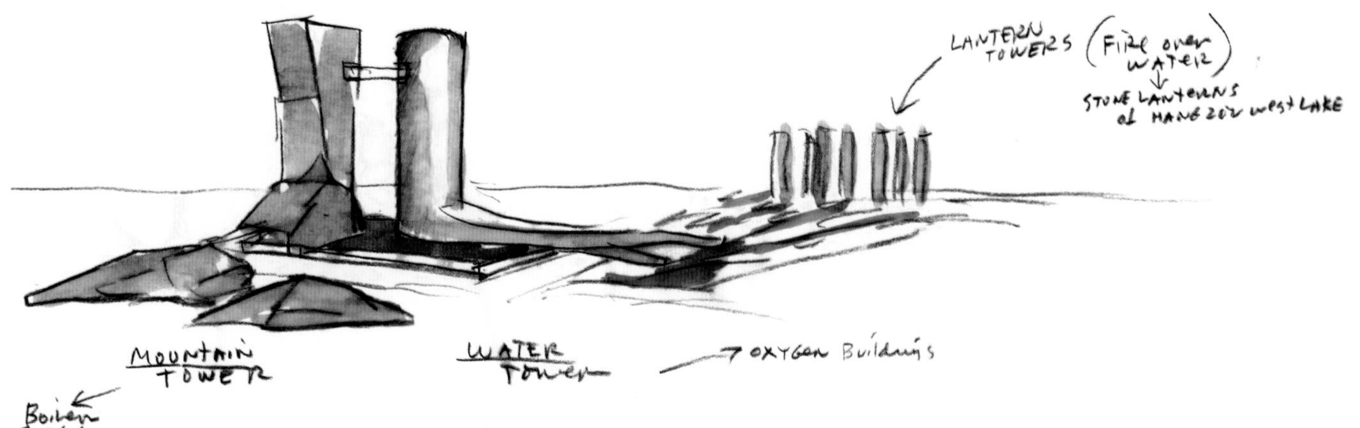

Heart of The NEW ZONE =
vertical GATHERING of The
Two ends of The "Bow TIE" plan
into MOUNTAIN & WATER SOUL of HANGZHOU

1/8/10 SIT

SHAN-SHUI HANGZHOU

Hangzhou, China
2010–14
Competition: First Place

Shan-Shui refers to the fusion of architecture and landscape at the core of this competition's winning design. This master plan, encompassing more than four million square feet (371,600 square meters) of new construction, connects existing factories to the north and south (to be rebuilt by Herzog & de Meuron and David Chipperfield based on the overall master plan by Steven Holl Architects).

A bow tie–shaped plan includes a water tower and mountain tower at the center, with tributary elements hovering between landform and architecture:

Canal Spreaders characterize a new zone of living by the water.

Lantern Towers, inspired by the stone lanterns of Hangzhou's freshwater lake West Lake, incorporate photovoltaic cells in special Fresnel glass.

The 3-D Park is a vertical fusion of gardens within gardens.

vimeo.com/307765010

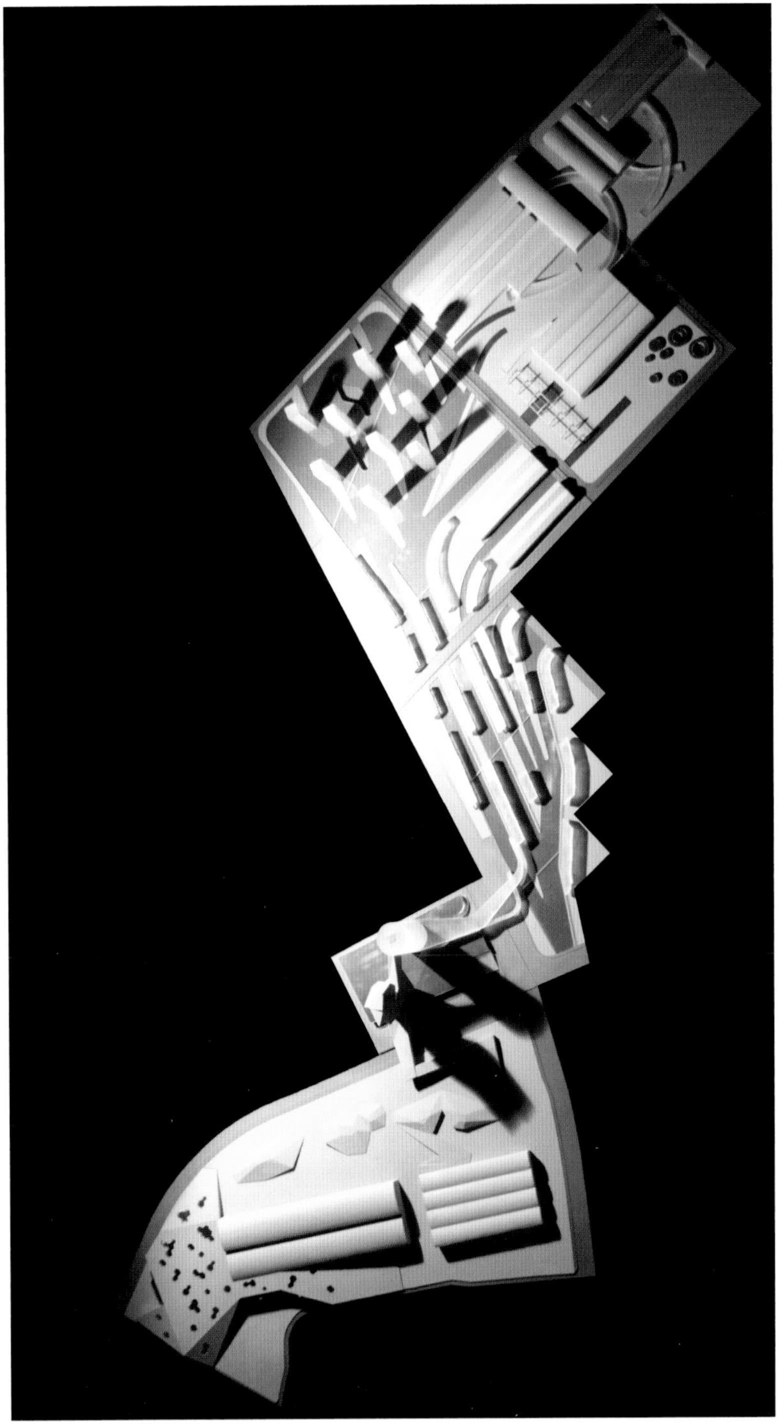

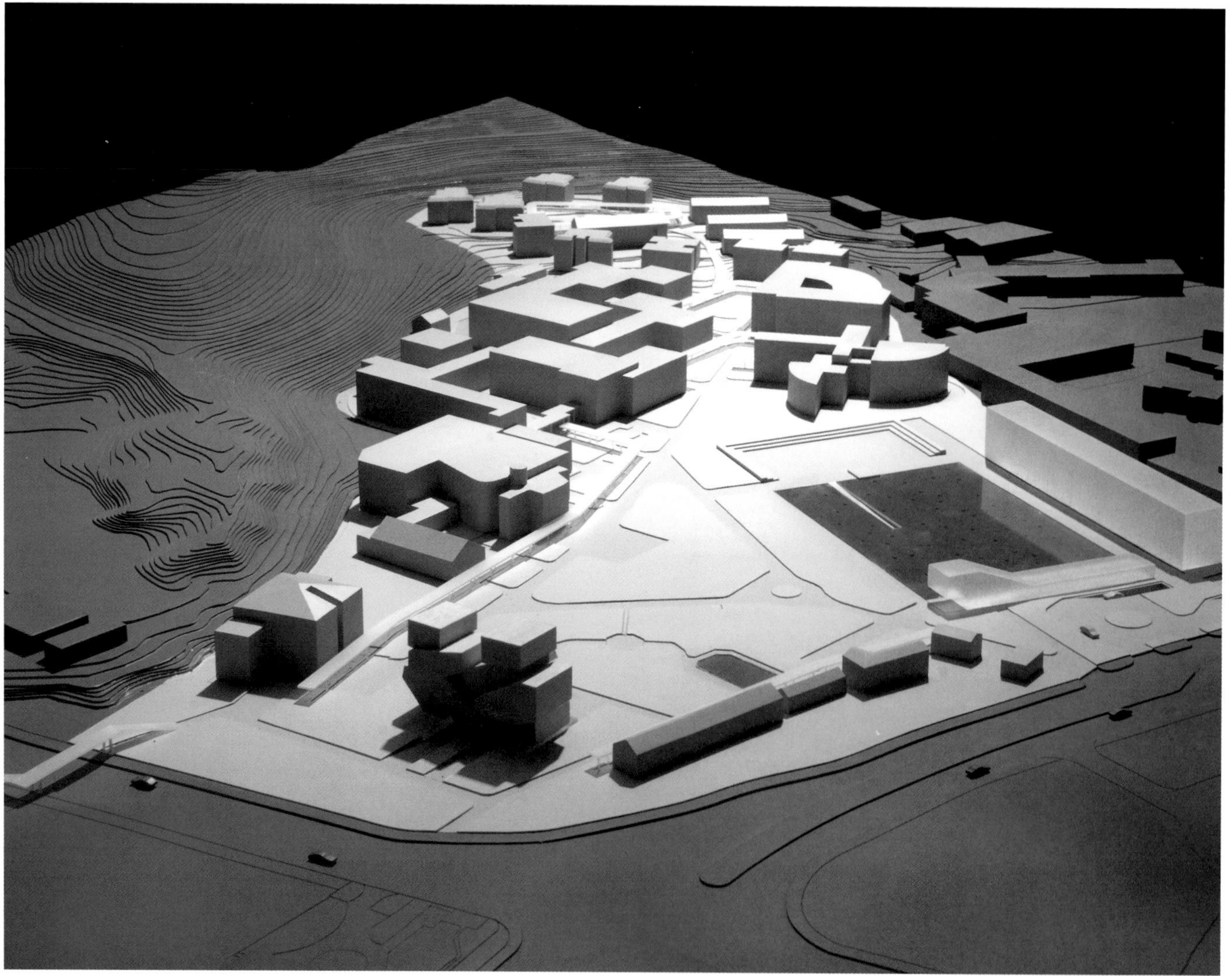

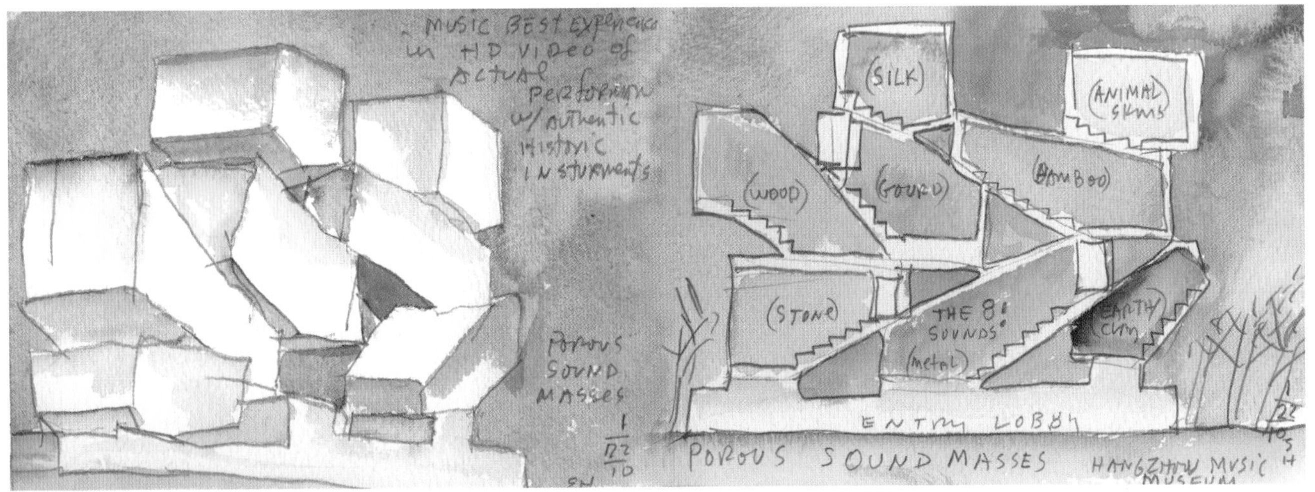

HANGZHOU MUSIC MUSEUM

Hangzhou, China
2010

As a stack of eight small auditoriums, the new Music Museum is based on the Eight Sounds of traditional Chinese music: silk, bamboo, wood, stone, metal, clay, gourd, and hide.

Each volume contains a chamber where visitors can not only hear music but experience its production. Interiors are developed with traditional materials.

The new Music Museum is part of a master plan reworking an existing campus via voids between buildings, like caesuras in music. A thin layer of water over the central plaza covers skylights to spaces below.

top
Concept drawing of the Eight Sounds

right
Music Museum at Water Plaza

VISUAL ARTS BUILDING
UNIVERSITY OF IOWA

Iowa City, Iowa, USA
2010–16
Competition: First Place

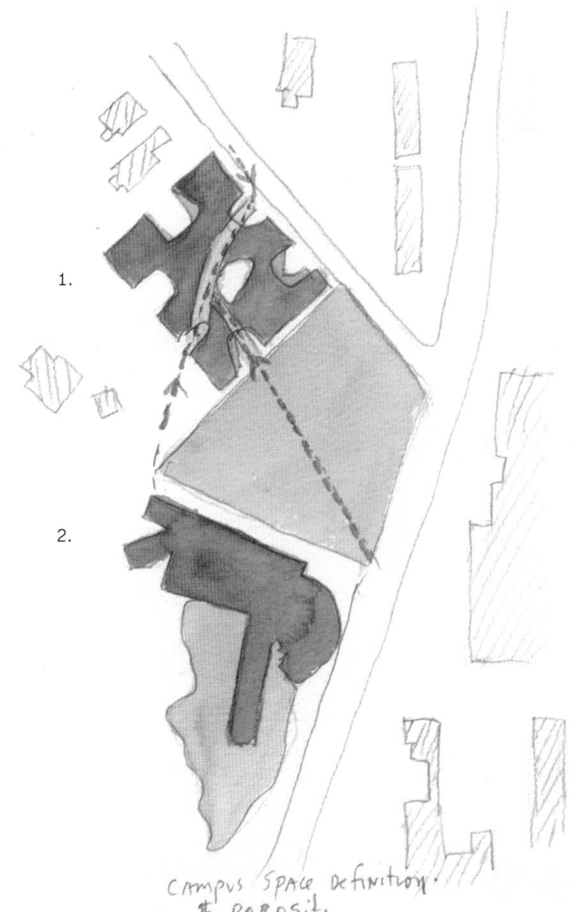

1. 2016 building
2. 2007 building
—
A new campus quadrangle green was formed with space reserved when the 2007 arts building engaged the quarry pond. Originally, the 2007 arts building was to be centered in what is now a campus space.

Due to a flood and FEMA funding, the rare chance to build another arts building adjacent to our Iowa Arts Building West (completed in 2007) presented a real challenge: How to make a new and larger arts building that would complement the first? The architectural language of the 2007 building was planar, executed in steel. We chose to build the new in contrast, based in a volumetric language and built in concrete.

The program encompasses 126,000 square feet (11,700 square meters) of loftlike space for the departments of ceramics, sculpture, metals, photography, printmaking, and 3-D multimedia. It also includes graduate student studios, faculty and staff studios, offices, and gallery space.

Presentation video: vimeo.com/190628857

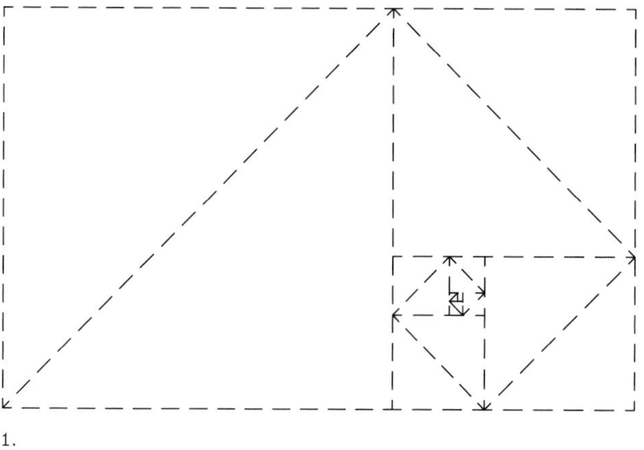

1.

2.

The Visual Arts Building employs two geometric operations: vertical cuts (multiple centers of light) and laminar shifts. The shift along floor lines creates balconies and imbues the vertical cuts with spatial energy. These two operations shape the four-story art school, which has a nearly square plan (288 feet [88 meters] on each side); natural light enters all interior spaces. The critically located vertical cuts, together with the laminar shift in the plane of each facade, compose a particular overall envelope modulated in geometric proportions.

above

1. Golden section proportions ordering all cuts and openings

2. Concept sketches, 2011

opposite

The central passage is a social condenser bringing all campus disciplines together.

1 Entry
2 Studio
3 Classroom
4 Forum
5 Office
6 Exhibition Space
7 Sculpture Court
8 Woodshop
9 Outdoor Kiln
10 Gallery

Fourth-floor plan 40'

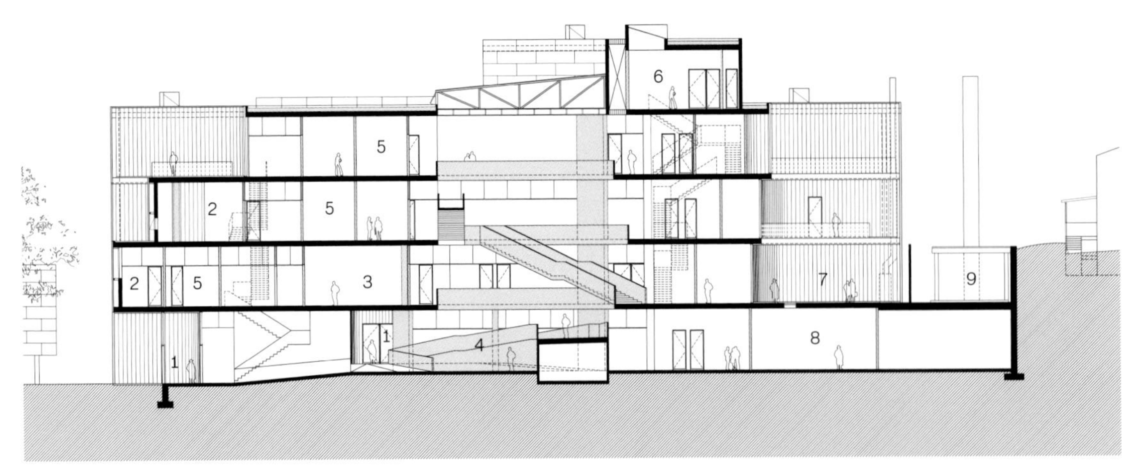

Section 40'

Multiple centers of light shape the plan to bring natural light to all rooms.

Stone Motorcycles sculpture by Mike Metz marks an entrance.

LONG ISLAND

HUNTERS POINT COMMUNITY LIBRARY

Long Island City, New York, USA
2010–19

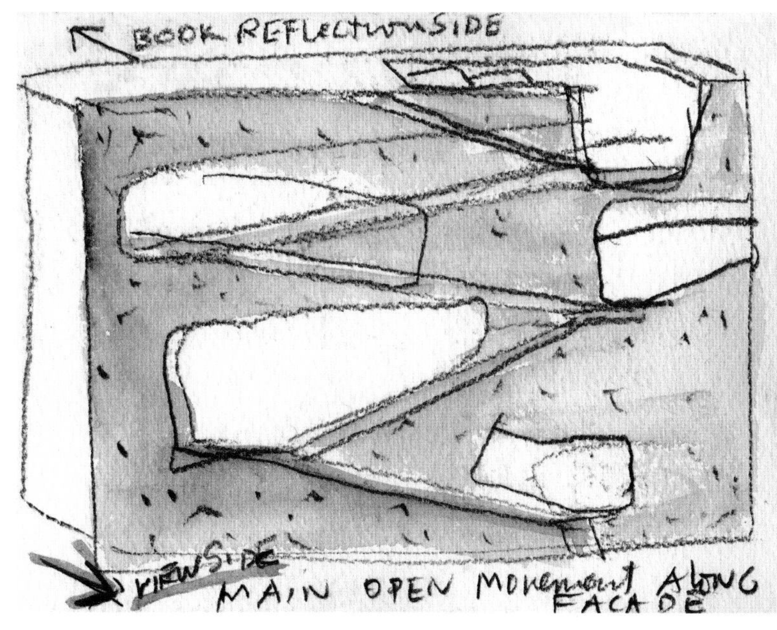

Located along the East River against the backdrop of recently built tower condominiums, the 22,000-square-foot (2,044-square-meter) Hunters Point Community Library in Queens stands as a public building and public reading garden. It brings community-devoted space to the increasingly privatized Long Island City waterfront. Deputy leader of the New York City Council, Jimmy Van Bramer, refused a developer's offer of free space in the two bottom levels of a proposed condominium tower, arguing for an entirely public building.

The Hunters Point Community Library is a sectionally developed, rectangular parallelepiped without interior columns. The concrete structure is exposed and characterizes all four elevations. The simple operation of rotational cuts in the thick, load-bearing concrete building envelope determines the building's inner space, inner light, and outward form. This series of cuts aligns with the circulation inside the building. The most prominent cut rotation traces the interior stairs to provide spectacular Manhattan views. This cut is perpendicular to tiers of bookshelves facing south, backed by linear computer desks on their north side, balancing the book and the digital.

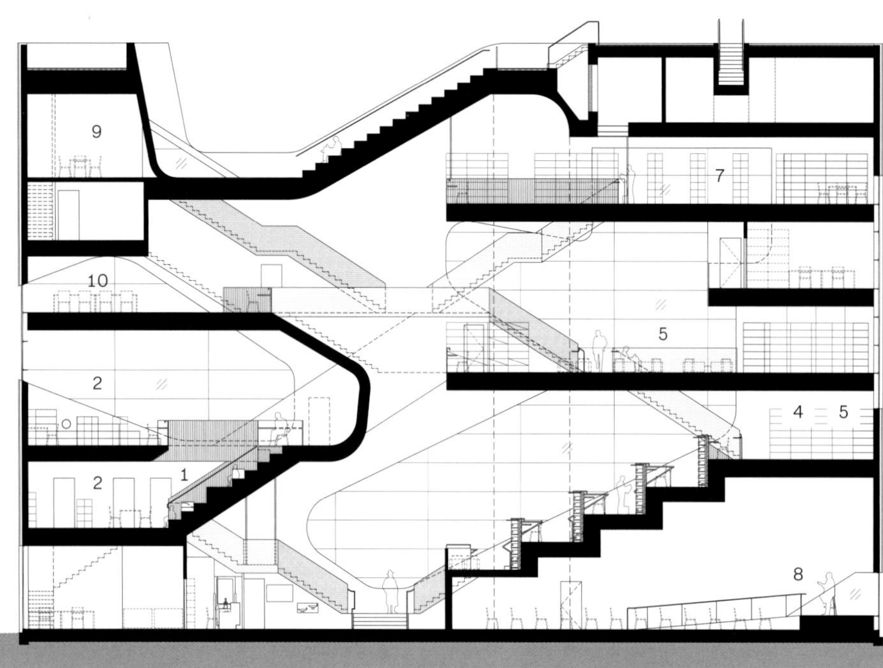

Section 20'

1 Children's Activities Area
2 Children's Area
3 Early Childhood Area
4 Periodicals
5 Adult Reading Collection
6 Media/E-Books
7 Teen Area
8 Meeting Room
9 Café
10 Cyber Center

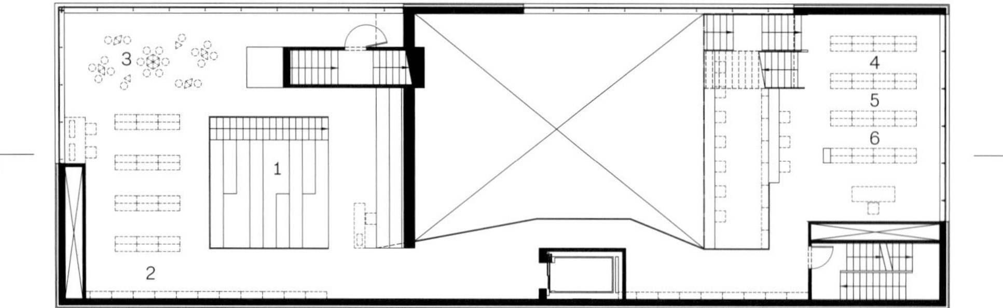

Second-floor plan 20'

First sketch of the Manhattan-view stair along the ascending bookcases. Behind each of the book stacks is a long computer counter, balancing the digital and analog.

The building's Manhattan face is cut at the children's area on right and rooftop café at top.

The program's division into children's, teen, and adult areas can be read in the sculpted openings of the east facade, which faces a reading garden bordered by a low park pavilion and a bosk of ginkgo trees.

Visitors can ascend to a rooftop café with a panoramic view of Manhattan.

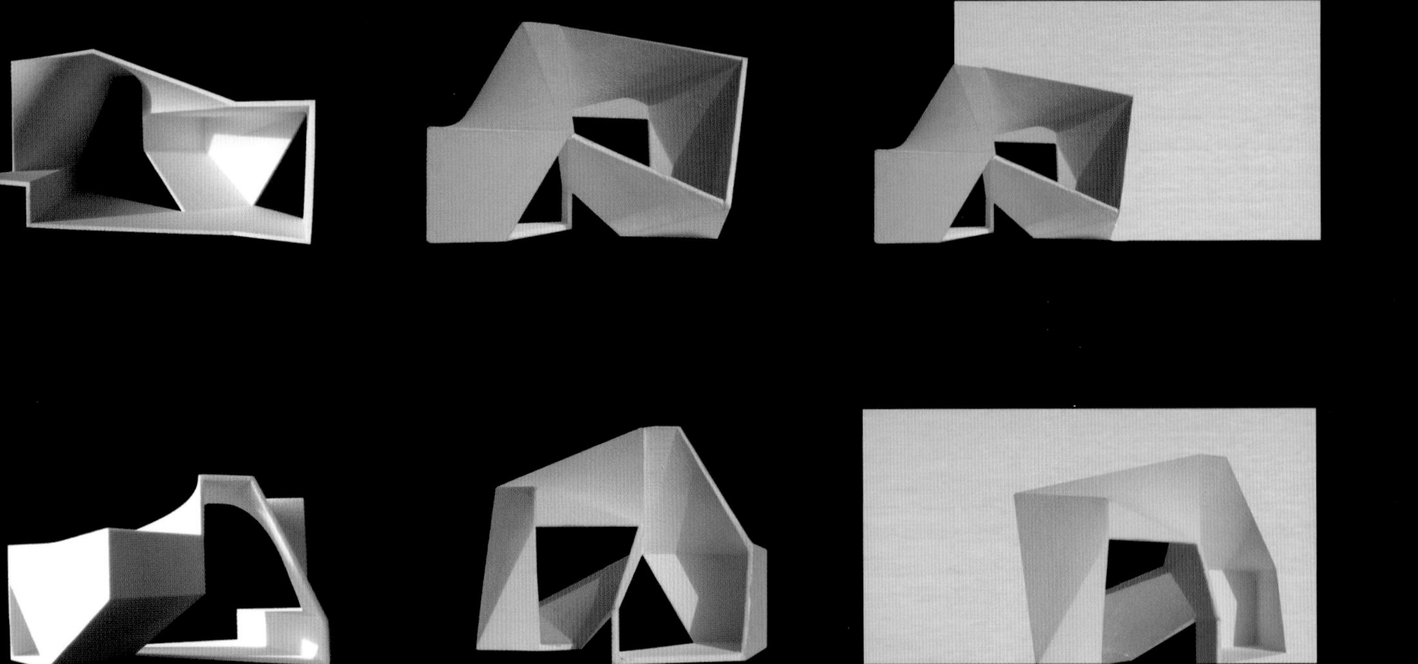

NEW DOCTORATE'S BUILDING NATIONAL UNIVERSITY OF COLOMBIA

Bogotá, Colombia
2010–

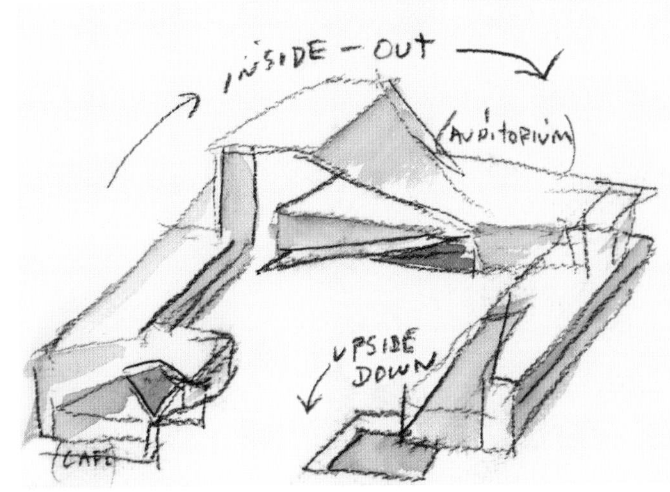

The New Doctorate's Building aligns with the university's 1930 master plan by Leopoldo Rother, a German Colombian urban planner and architect. Organized as an ellipse and divided into five parts, the plan was eroded in the 1970s. Our building reestablishes the original plan morphology.

The moderate climate of Bogotá (cool summers and temperate winters) allows for space turned inside out to an open-air section at the heart of the new building. The life of the school, with students moving back and forth on exterior walks, is centered around this open social space.

From the building's six-hundred-seat auditorium, the roof begins to warp upward, shaping a campus gate–like pergola. Here, sun-protected social space is aligned to one of the original diagonals of the 1930 master plan.

The south arm of the building rises up in a cantilevered restaurant with roof terraces and mountain views. The north arm turns down into the landscape, opening to an "upside-down" portion that shapes a grotto water garden. Continuous flows of rain water and gray water are linked in this lower basin; a reflecting pool at the auditorium emits the sound of slowly pouring water.

The water recycling system is driven by solar photovoltaic cells on the roof, which also provide 15 percent of the electrical power for the new structure. High-performance reinforced concrete joins local wood and Bogotá stone in a palette of material resonance and ecological innovation.

All construction drawings are complete, and construction is slated to start between 2019 and 2021. As of this writing, it has been eight years since we began design… Architecture takes time.

opposite
Study models, 2011

above
Concept sketch, 2011

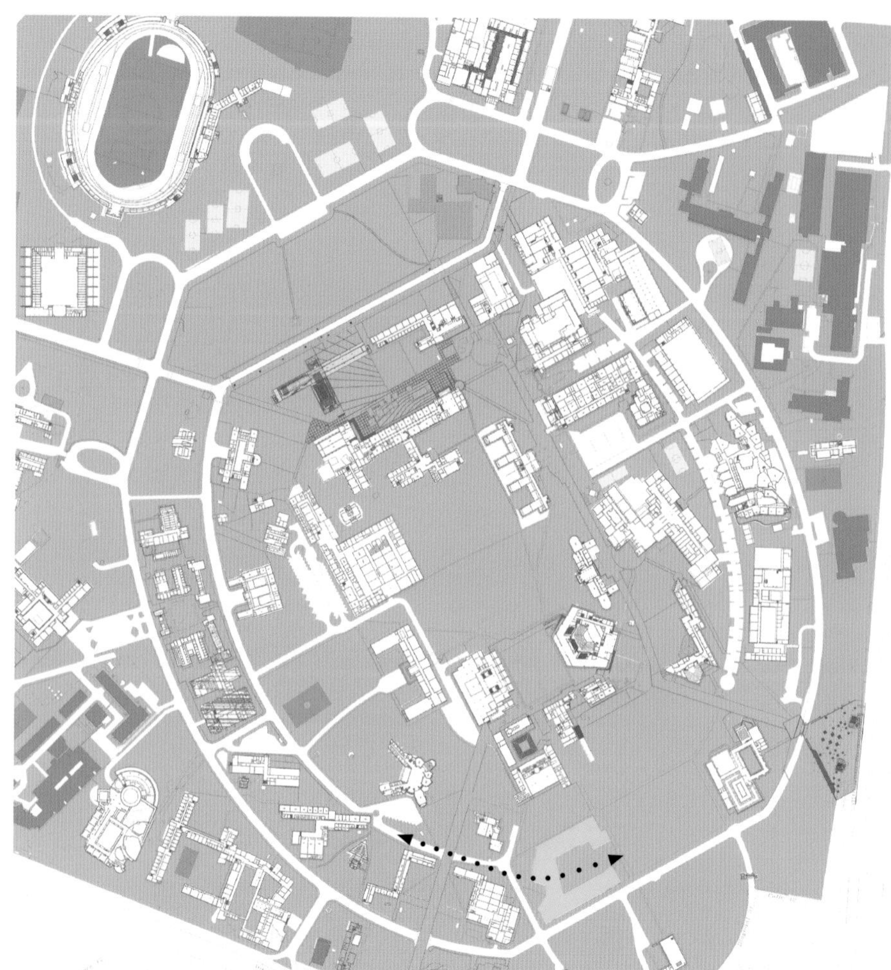

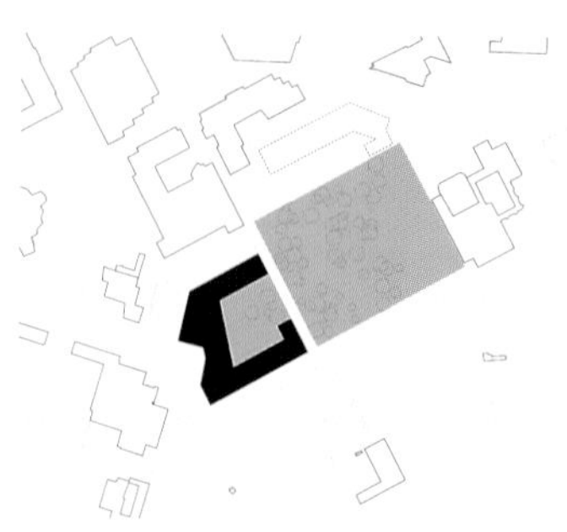

Shaping green space

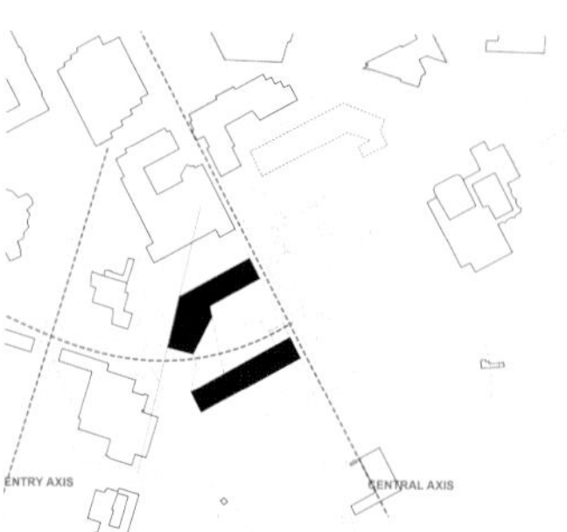

Linking campus entry and central axis

1 Covered Courtyard
2 Lobby
3 Reflecting Pool
4 Auditorium
5 Study Area
6 Student Collaboration Rooms
7 Classrooms

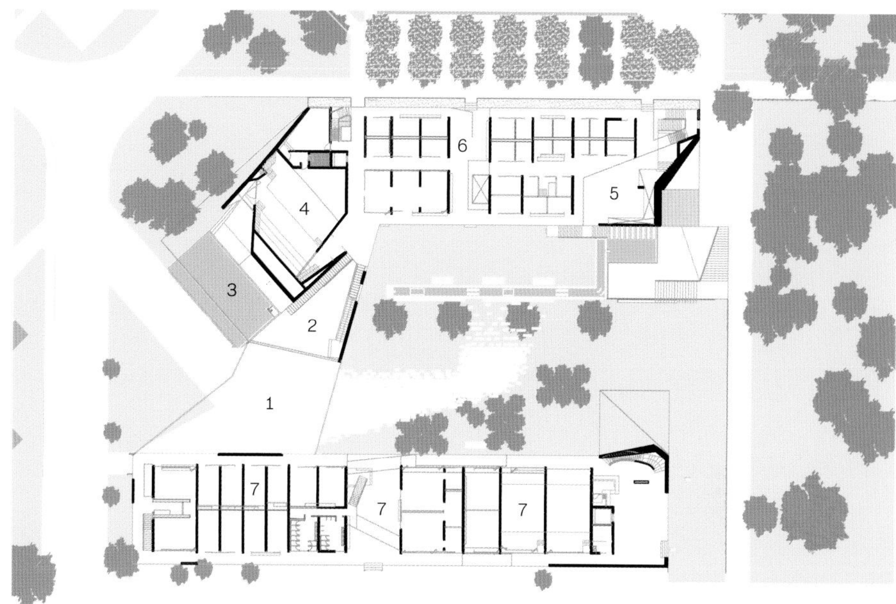

Central open-air pergola. The concept of a gradual turn from inside out to upside down will be built in white titanium concrete.

INSTITUTE FOR CONTEMPORARY ART VIRGINIA COMMONWEALTH UNIVERSITY

Richmond, Virginia, USA
2011–18
Competition: First Place

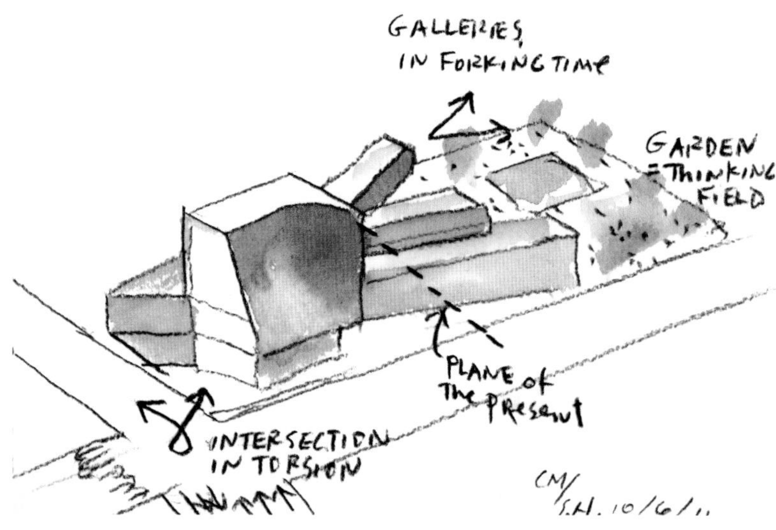

Sited at the edge of the Virginia Commonwealth University campus in Richmond, Virginia, the new Institute for Contemporary Art links the university with the surrounding community. On the busiest intersection of Richmond, at Broad and Belvidere Streets, the building forms a gateway to the university.

The street entrance is formed by a joining of the performance space and forum, adding a *z* component to the *x/y* movement of the intersection. The torsion of these connecting bodies is joined by a "plane of the present" to the galleries in "forking time."

The forking time concept of the ICA is a reflection on our era in art, when there is no longer one grand narrative.

Unlike in the 1950s, when abstract painting was a dominant movement, or in the 1960s, when conceptual art and minimalism dominated, today we experience art as a "garden of forking paths," in the words of Jorge Luis Borges in the 1941 story of that name: "It is not space, but time which forks."

This notion is expressed in a forking split, where four main galleries diverge (one vertically). This brachiating or bifurcating geometry is anchored by a plane of the present—a vertical light catcher uniting the upward and downward shift of forms on the northeast with the splitting spatial transformation of the southwest.

The building has two fronts—one on the city side and one on the campus side, opening to the sculpture garden.

Presentation video: vimeo.com/204033729

opposite
The new building's geometry responds to the city's busiest intersection and forms a gateway to the campus.

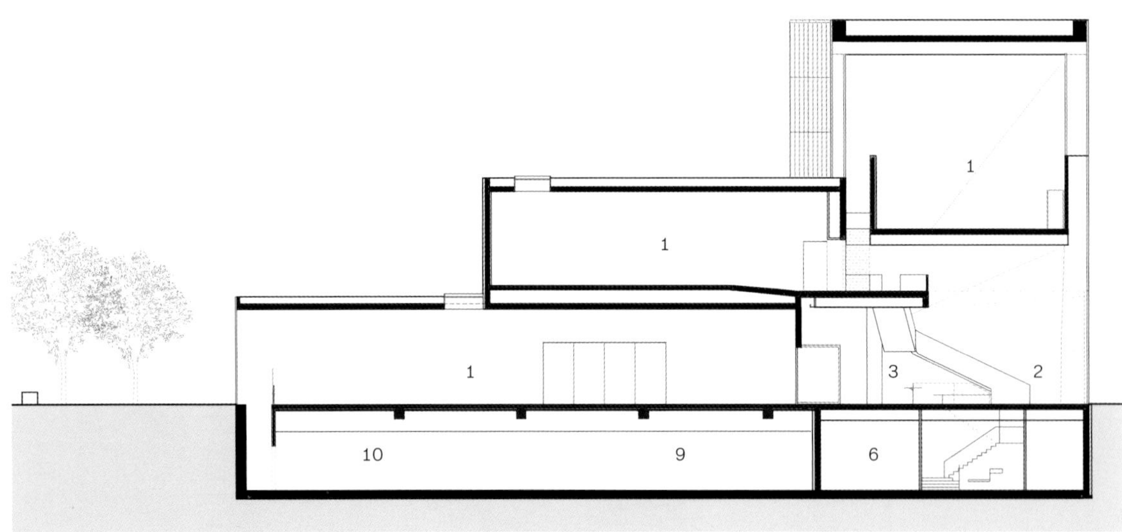

Section A  40'

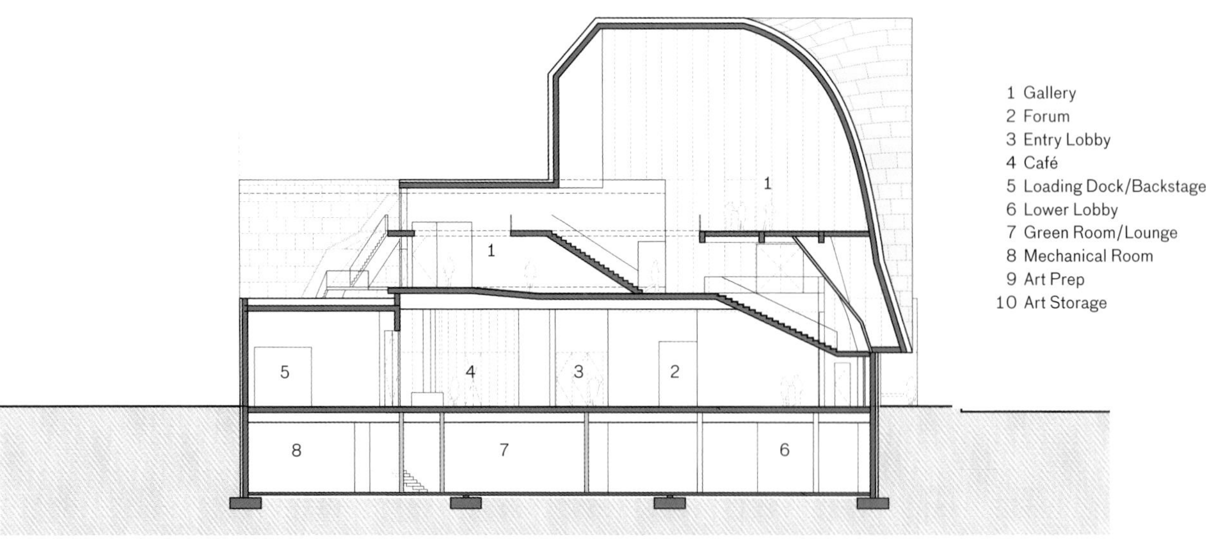

Section B 40'

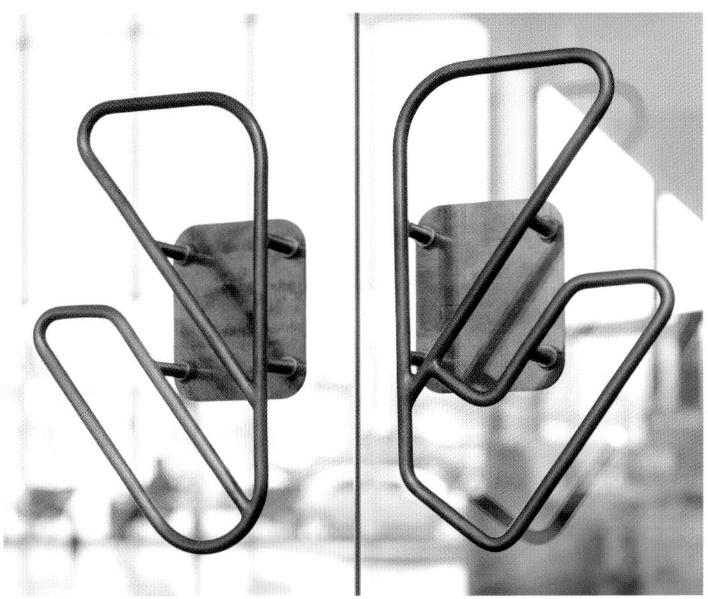

above
The forum and the entrance facing downtown Richmond

right
Bronze door handles in a version of an ampersand

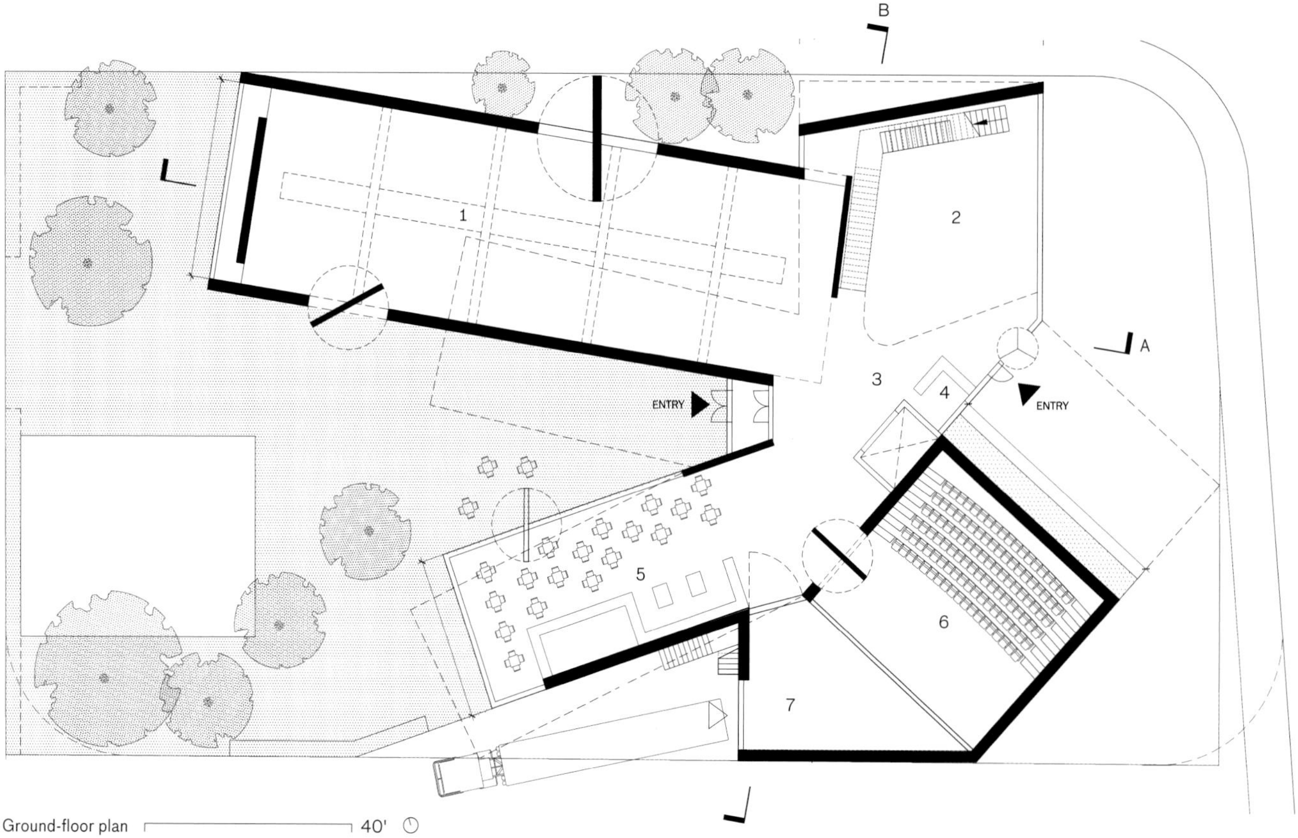

Ground-floor plan 40'

1 Gallery
2 Forum
3 Entry Lobby
4 Reception
5 Café
6 Performance Space
7 Loading Dock

above
The two entrances—one from the garden, one from the street intersection—activate the lobby.

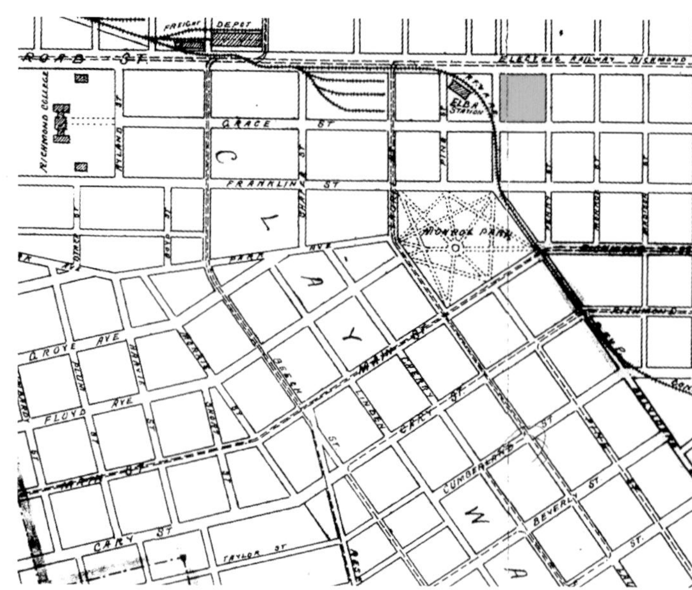

right
The history of the site, at the center of Richmond, includes the forking track lines of the main train station.

The sculpture garden and pool form a quiet thinking field opposite the urban entrance at the central intersection of Richmond.

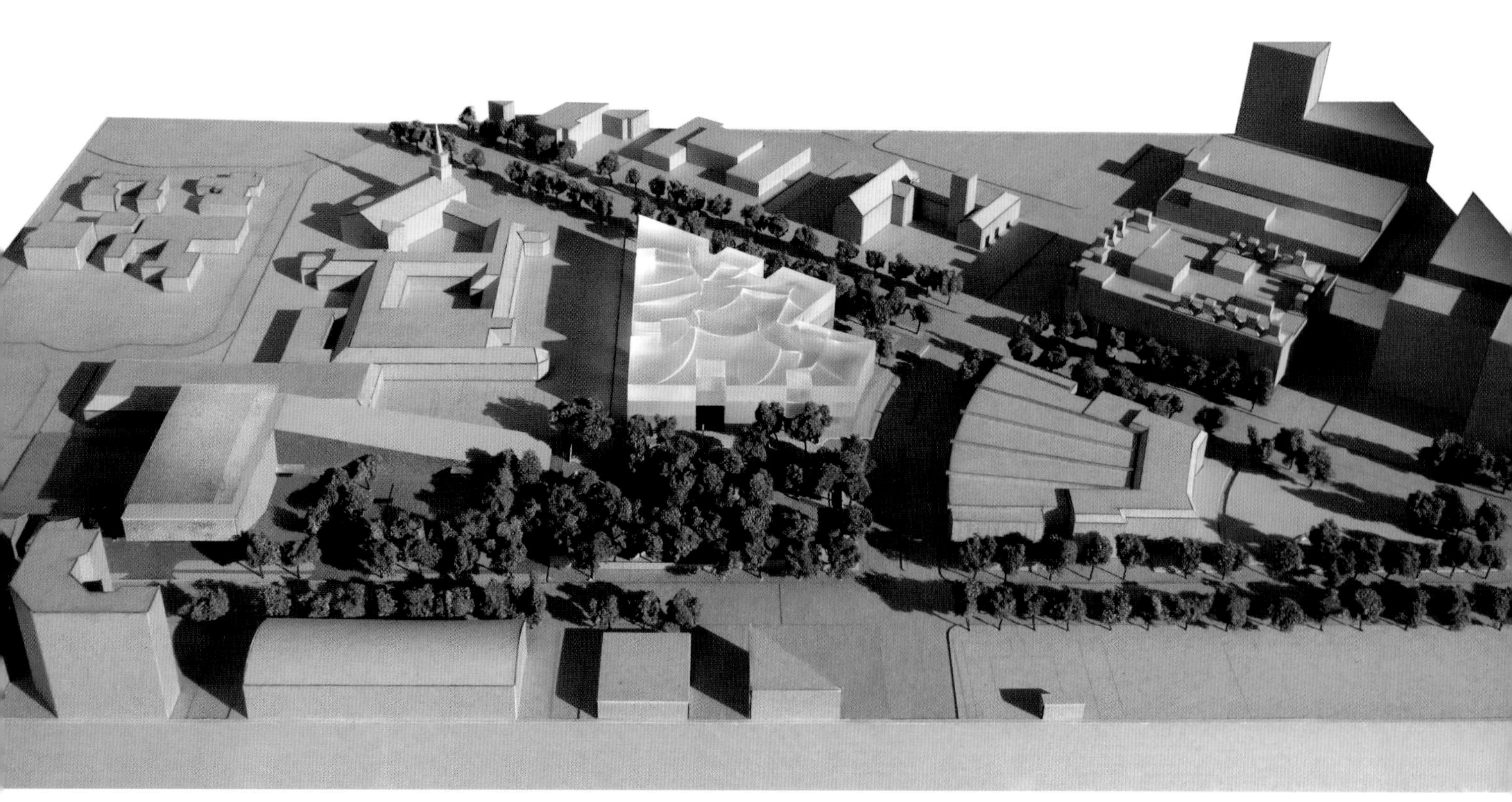

MUSEUM OF FINE ARTS, HOUSTON CAMPUS EXPANSION

Houston, Texas, USA

2011–

Competition: First Place

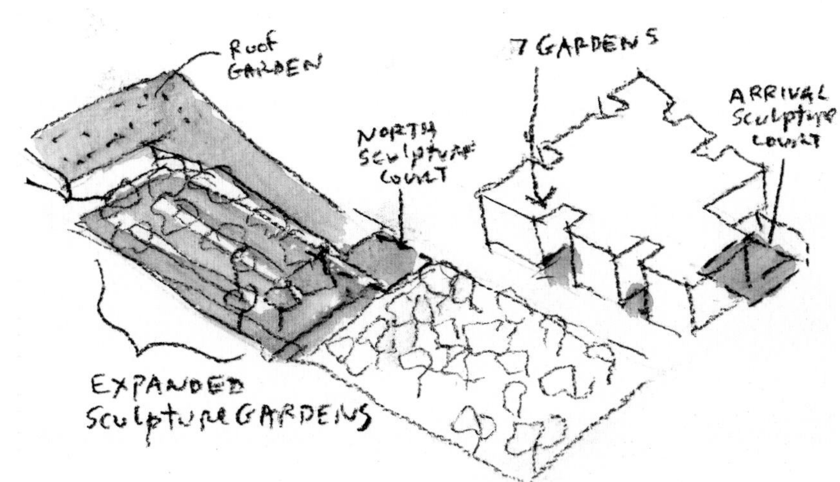

2011 competition concept sketch showing no parking garage (a continuous underground level of parking), a new Glassell School, and enlarged sculpture garden

The international competition for the expansion of the Museum of Fine Arts, Houston, began in 2011 with a list of ten competitors and was reduced to a short list of three finalists. We made our final presentation to the MFAH board on January 27, 2012. The program required a seven-story parking garage, which would replace an existing parking lot where the new museum pavilion was to be located. We argued that this moment instead presented the potential for an MFAH campus, via an underground layer of parking, a new 93,000-square-foot (8,640-square-meter) Glassell School of Art, and a doubling of the Isamu Noguchi–designed sculpture garden (our scheme required the demolition of the 40,000-square-foot [3,716 square-meter] Glassell Building from 1979).

We suggested that the museum was at a crossroads moment, not unlike a train running down a track. With a simple turn of the switch, a more campuslike facility could be established (along with a sculpture garden slightly larger than that of the Dallas Museum of Art). The jury vote was unanimous.

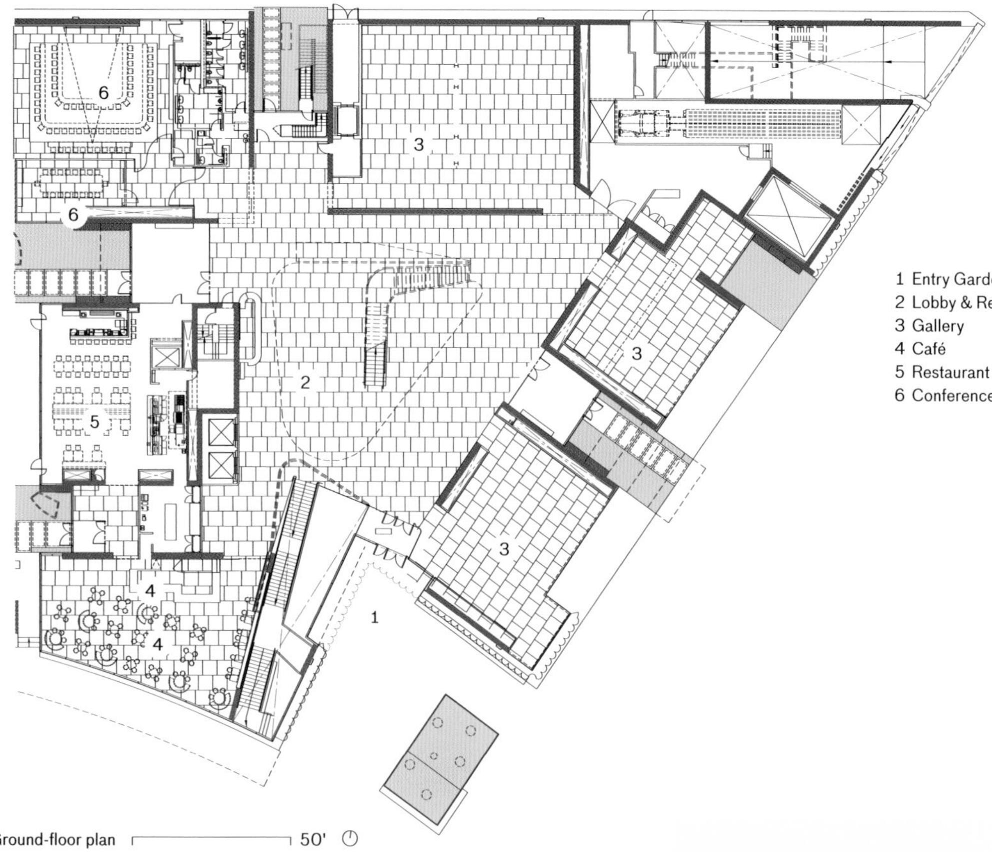

1 Entry Garden
2 Lobby & Reception
3 Gallery
4 Café
5 Restaurant
6 Conference Room

Ground-floor plan 50'

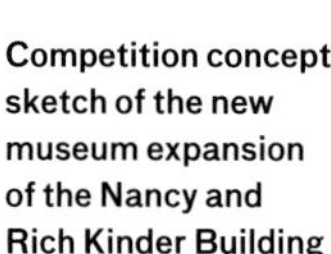

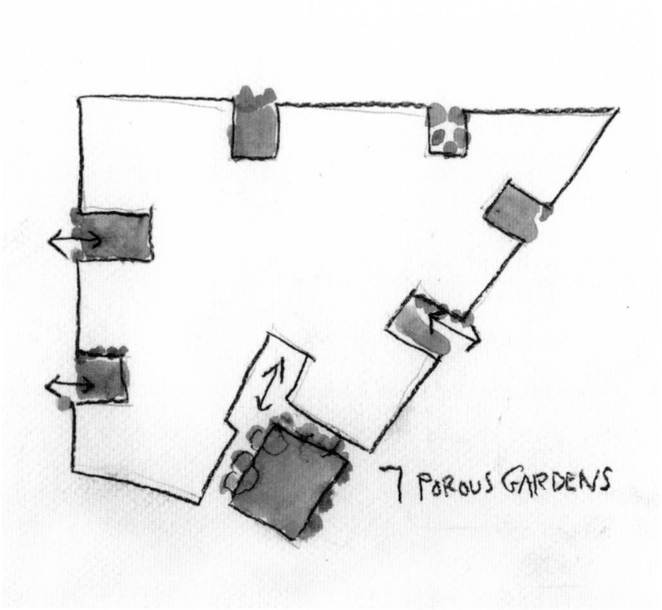

POROUS GARDENS

Competition concept sketch of the new museum expansion of the Nancy and Rich Kinder Building

Competition sketch
of the Luminous Canopy

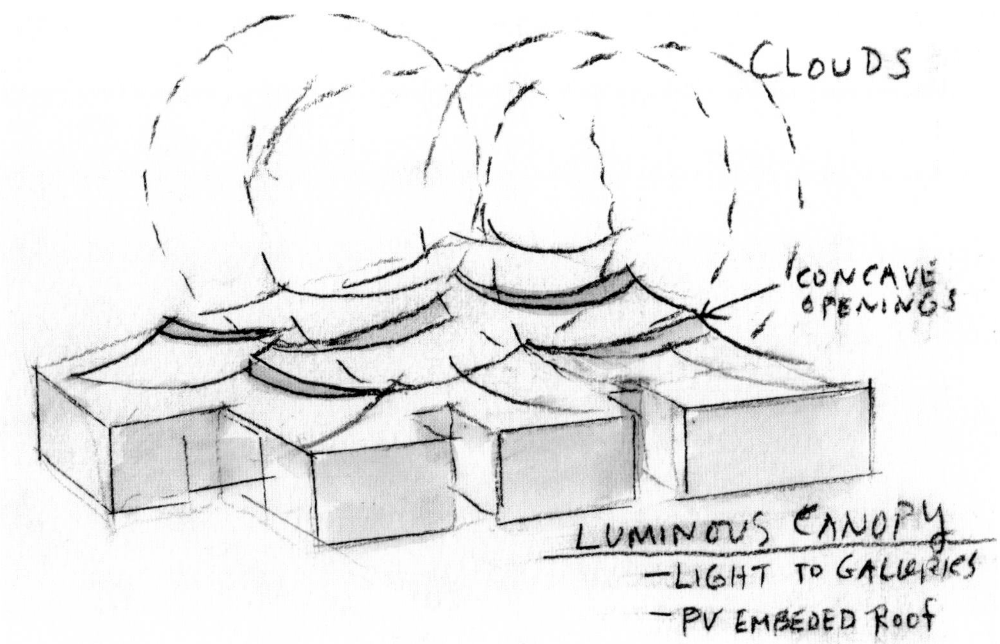

GLASSELL SCHOOL OF ART

Houston, Texas, USA
2011–18

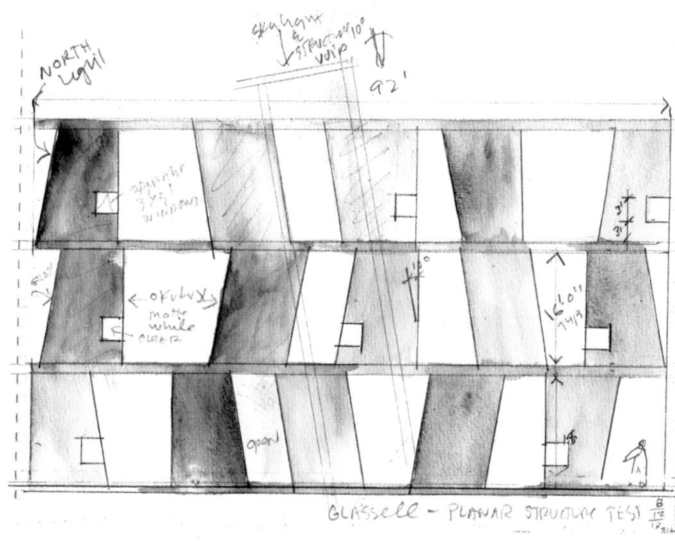

This new building for the school of art exists as the direct result of our winning the international competition for the new Museum of Fine Arts, Houston master plan.

In the original 1924 mission of the Museum of Fine Arts, Houston, art education is a primary emphasis. The decision to build the Glassell School of Art reflects the museum's original values.

The new L-shaped Glassell School defines the Brown Foundation Plaza and expands the Noguchi-designed sculpture garden.

The inclined plane of the roof forms an amphitheater and a public path to a rooftop garden overlooking the whole MFAH campus.

The building contains three gallery spaces:

1. one at ground level, near the cafe space overlooking the plaza;
2. one at the Education Court, connecting to the future Nancy and Rich Kinder Building through a sculpture tunnel;
3. one at the top of the forum, on the second floor; the main entry opens to a cascade of levels at a forum located where the two sides of the L meet, shaping an informal learning space directly opening to a seventy-seat auditorium.

The simple, planar structural pieces of sandblasted concrete begin with the angle of the inclined roof plane and give character to the inner spaces of the building in the spirit of simplicity and directness inherent in Mies van der Rohe's original building across the street. The concrete planes alternate with large, translucent panels to provide ideal, diffuse light to the studios. As an educational building, it instructs us in how it is made.

above
Structural concept sketch, 2013. Every studio has an operable square window.

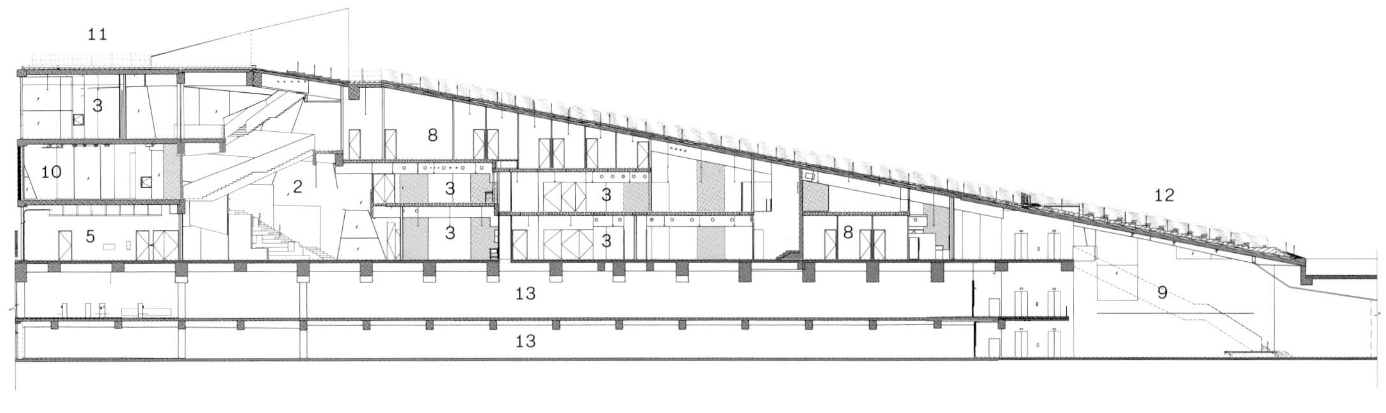

Section 40'

1 Entry
2 Forum
3 Studio
4 Auditorium
5 Workshop
6 Exhibition Space
7 Café
8 Office
9 Education Court
10 Gallery
11 Roof Garden
12 Amphitheater
13 Parking

Ground-floor plan 40'

above
Precast concrete facade pieces act as a structure, supporting the floors. The concrete was cast in Waco, Texas, and set in place by crane. The heaviest panel weighs 40,046 lbs. (18,165 kg), a lift-up record.

right
The forum space central to the L-shaped plan.

North Wing
(Great Hall)
MAGGIES
East Wing
King George V
Building (KGV)

MAGGIE'S CENTRE BARTS

London, United Kingdom
2011–17

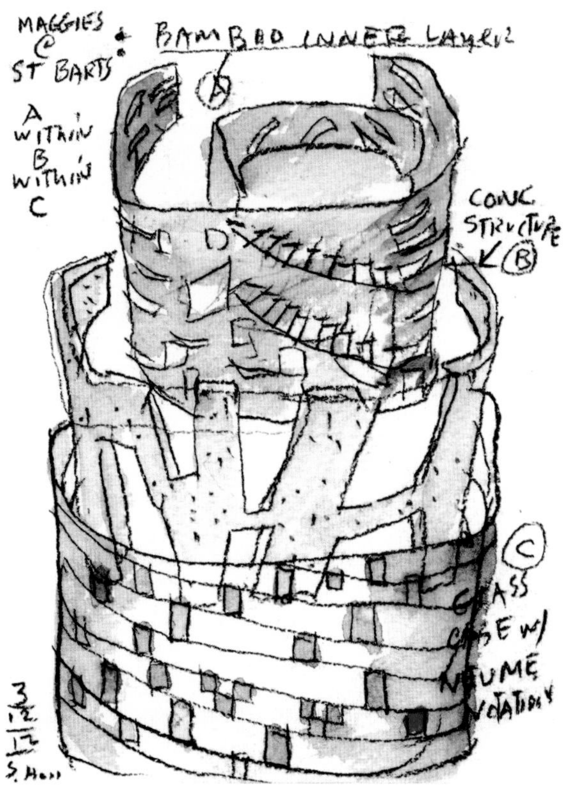

This site in Smithfield, in the center of London, is adjacent to the large courtyard of St. Bartholomew's Hospital, the oldest hospital in London. St. Bartholomew's was founded in the twelfth century, at the same time that the monk Rahere founded St. Bartholomew the Great Church "for the restoration of poor men." Layers of history characterize this unique site, connecting deeply to the medieval culture of London.

Maggie's is a charity that supports cancer patients and their family and friends. While nearly all of the realized Maggie's Centres have been horizontal buildings, the facility at Barts is vertical. It replaces a pragmatic 1960s brick structure and responds to an adjacent eighteenth-century stone structure by James Gibbs, preserving the older building's great hall and famous William Hogarth staircase.

The building is envisioned as a vessel within a vessel within a vessel. The structure is a branching concrete frame; its inner layer is perforated bamboo, and the outer layer is matte white glass with colored fragments recalling the neume notation of thirteenth-century medieval music. The word *neume* originates from the Greek *pnevma*, which means "vital force." It suggests a breath of life that fills one with inspiration, like a stream of air or the blowing of the wind. The outer glass layer is organized in horizontal bands like a musical staff, while the concrete structure branches like the hand.

Presentation video: vimeo.com/65395492

above
Concept sketch, 2012

opposite
The stained glass is a new type we invented with the company Okalux.

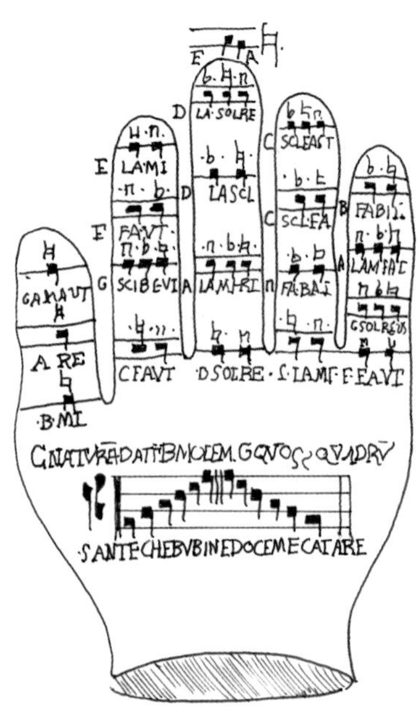

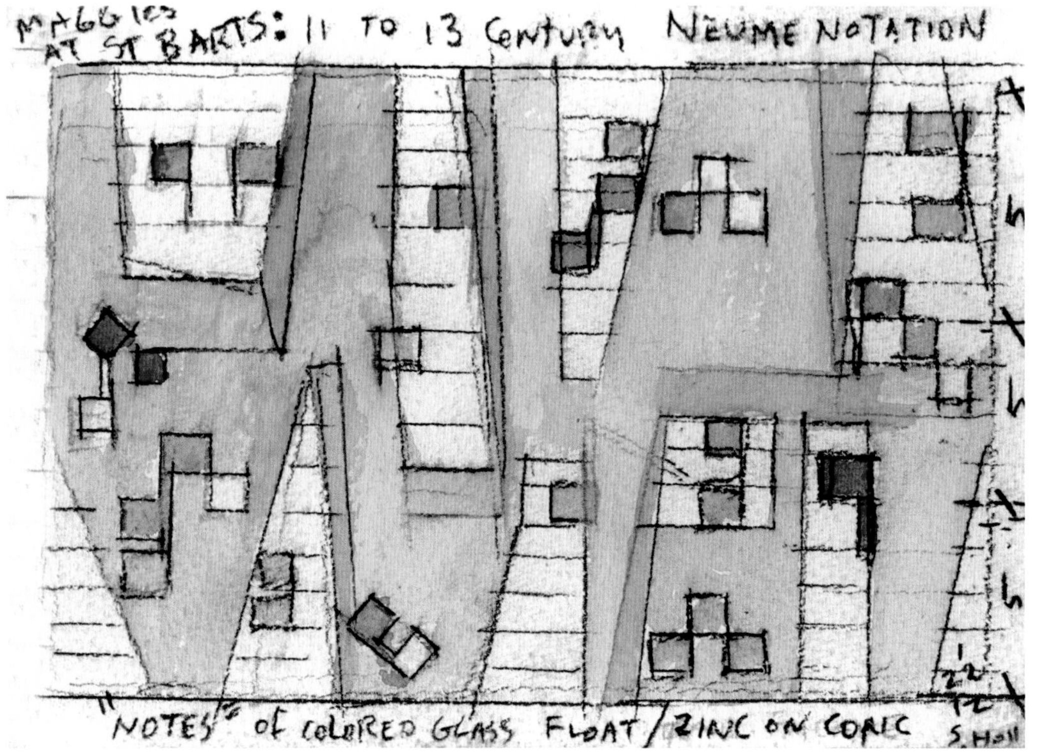

top
Twelfth-century neume notation and staff

left
Early concept sketch uniting the concrete structure

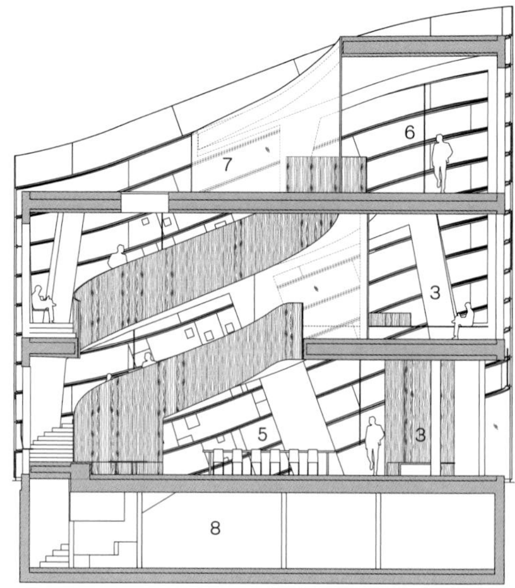

Section 5m

1 Entry
2 Pause Space
3 Counseling
4 Kitchen
5 Dining Table
6 Group Activity Room
7 Roof Garden
8 Plant Room

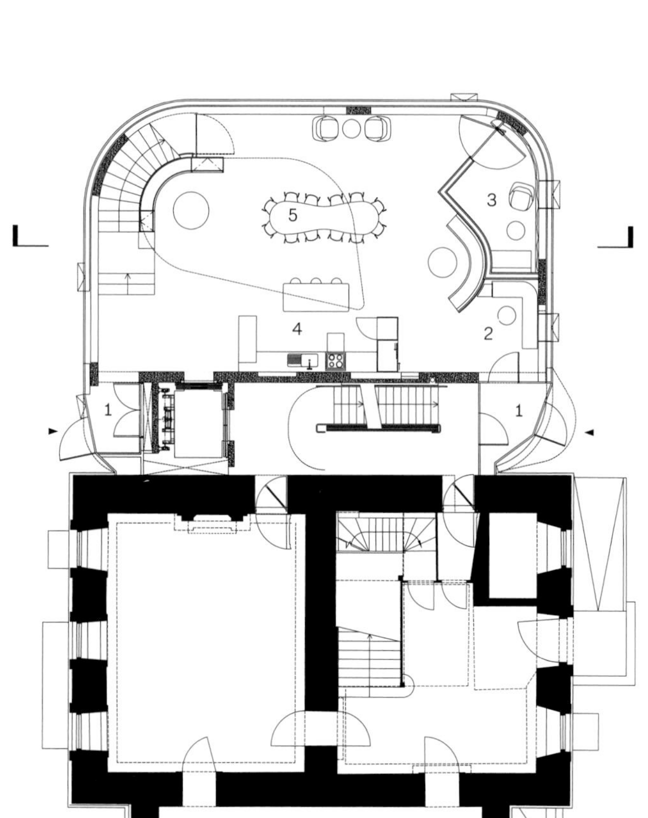

Ground-floor plan 5m

above
Section showing how the movement inside is parallel to the exterior musical staff—all culminating in the light of the roof garden

left
Thick and thin: the James Gibbs 1743 stone building with the 2017 Maggie's Centre in complementary contrast

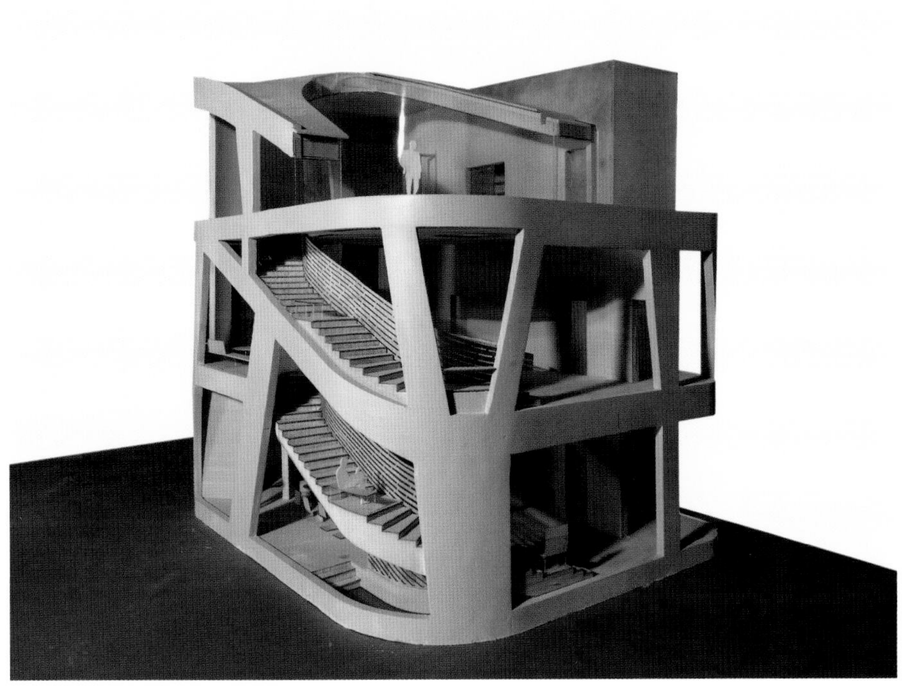

above
The concrete structure, which branches like a hand, is exposed inside.

right
Exposed concrete structure and natural bamboo along the neume notation in Okalux glass

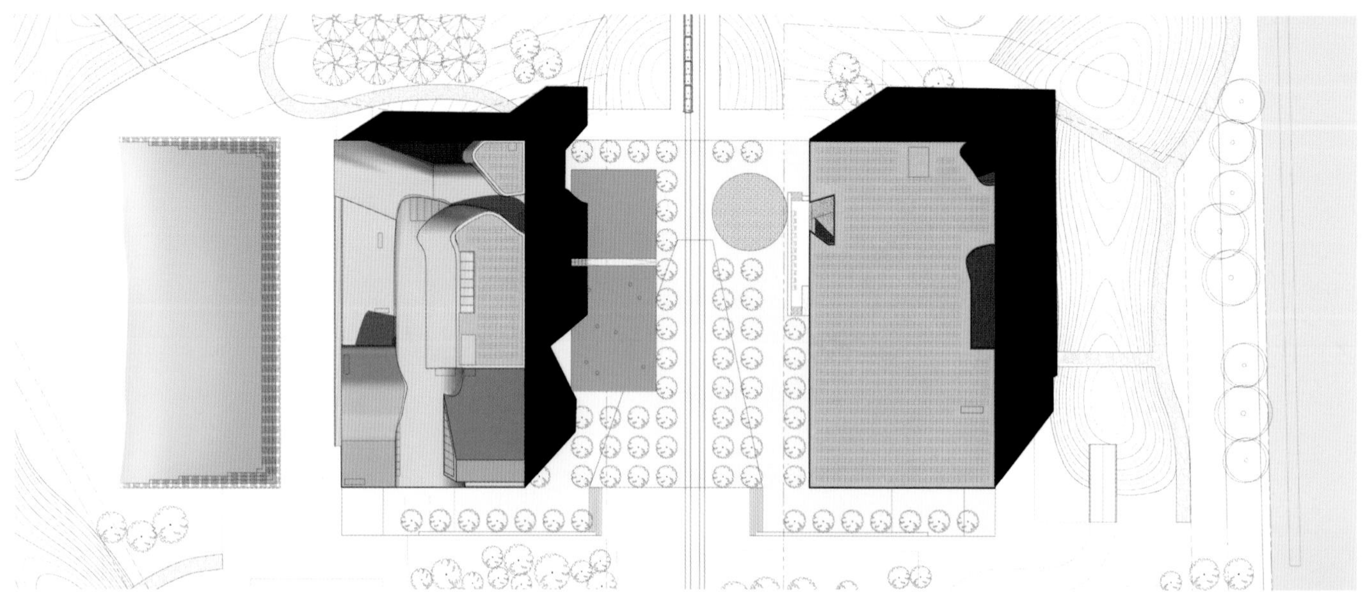

TIANJIN ECO-CITY ECOLOGY AND PLANNING MUSEUMS

Tianjin, China
2012–14
Competition: First Place

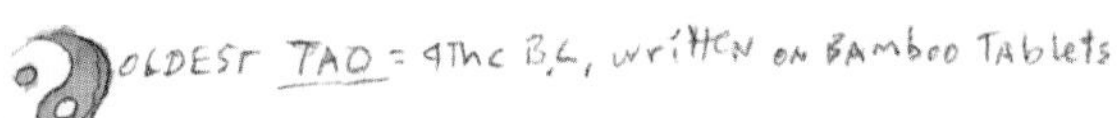

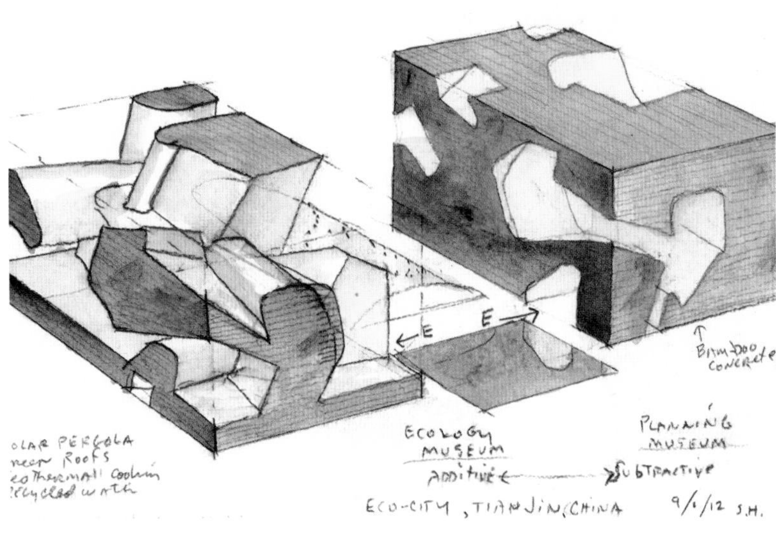

On reclaimed salt pan and polluted tide flats at Bohai Bay, China (a two-hour drive from Beijing), a new city for 350,000 inhabitants is being built from scratch. Founded as a collaboration of the governments of Singapore and China, this new eco-city was created to demonstrate state-of-the-art sustainable living.

The Ecology and Planning Museums are the first two buildings of the cultural district of Eco-City, Tianjin. The Planning Museum is a subtractive space, while the Ecology Museum is an additive complement, a reversal of space carved out from the Planning Museum. Like the Chinese *ba gua* or yin and yang, these forms are in reverse relations.

Each museum will be 215,000 square feet (20,000 square meters), with a service zone connecting them below grade, bringing the total construction to 650,000 square feet (60,000 square meters). A high-speed tram running between the two museums connects them to the central business district of Eco-City.

The design, which won a Progressive Architecture Award, had been executed through construction drawings and on-site construction mock-ups when the government changed in 2014, eliminating the mayor in charge and thereby canceling the building after three years of work.

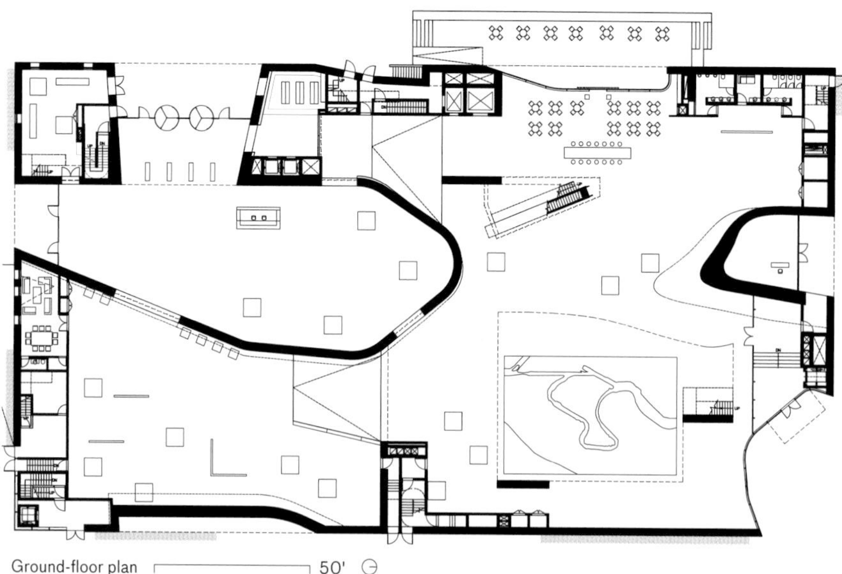

Ground-floor plan 50'

Ecology Museum: Bamboo-formed concrete sets the frame for subtractive and additive operations to take place.

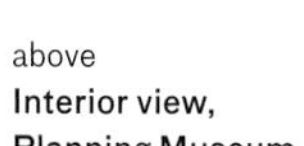

above
Interior view, Planning Museum

right
Sanded-aluminum and white-ceramic-tile tests from project team visit in March 2014

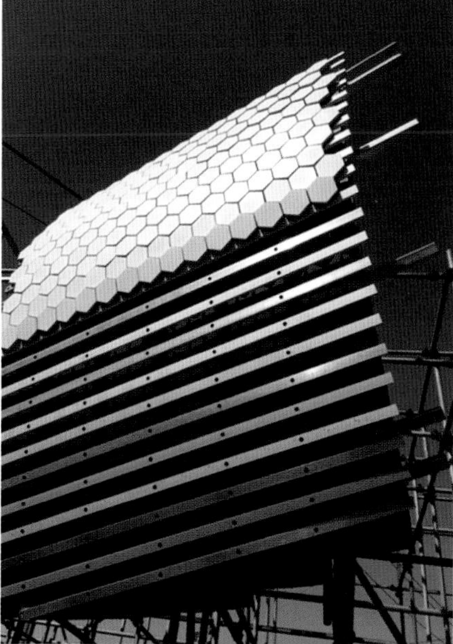

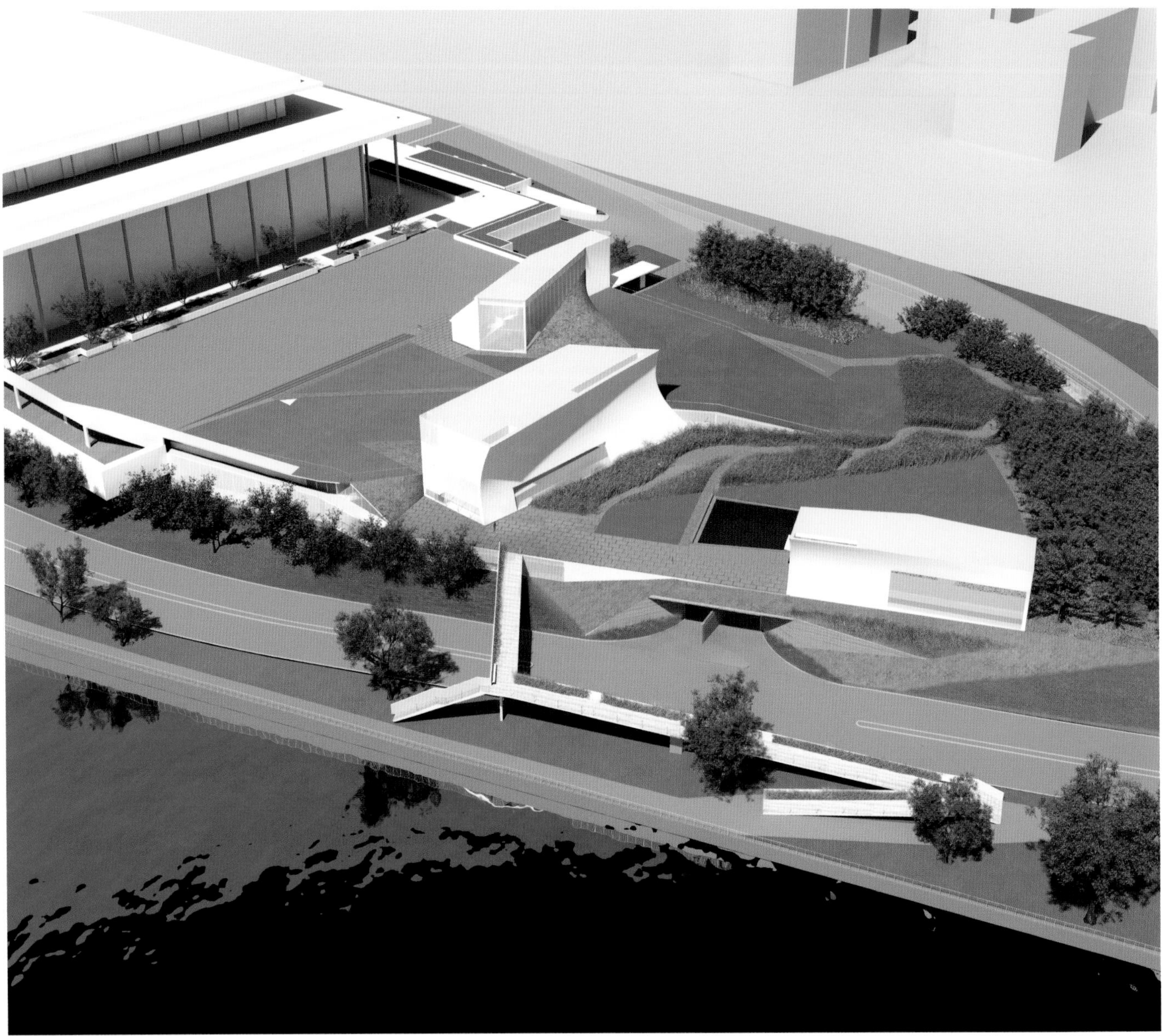

JOHN F. KENNEDY CENTER FOR THE PERFORMING ARTS EXPANSION

Washington, DC, USA

2012–19

Competition: First Place

To increase respect for the creative individual, to widen participation by all the processes and fulfillments of art—this is one of the fascinating challenges of these days.

—JOHN F. KENNEDY, 1962

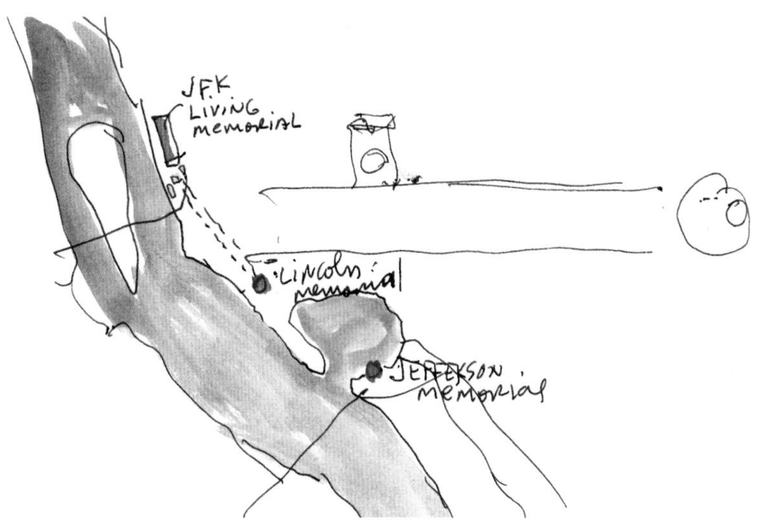

As the living memorial that bears the former president's name, the John F. Kennedy Center for the Performing Arts fulfills a vital mission by presenting and producing the best of the performing arts, supporting the creation of new works, and providing innovative and comprehensive arts education to millions of people across the country.

The new extension, 60 percent below ground, brings natural light to all spaces via three pavilions set into new gardens. Rehearsal, education, and a variety of flexible indoor and outdoor spaces will allow the center to continue to play a national and global leadership role in providing artistic, cultural, and enrichment opportunities for all.

Presentation video: vimeo.com/67599522

Unlike still monuments to Lincoln and Jefferson, the John F. Kennedy Center is an active place with over 365 programs a year.

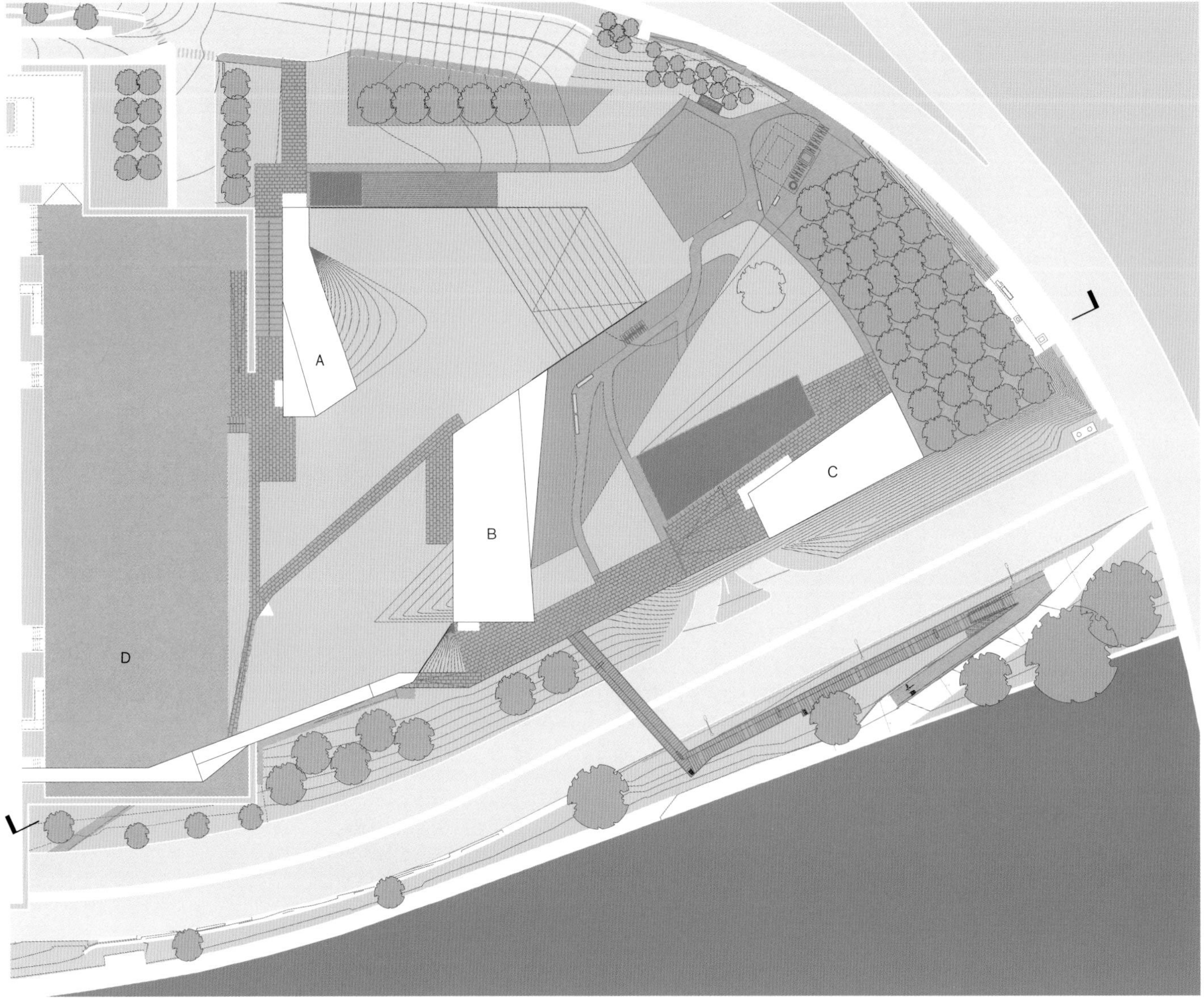

Site plan 50m

A Entry Pavilion
B Glissando Pavilion
C River Pavilion
D Existing Edward D. Stone Building Upper South Terrace

1 Event Space
2 Rehearsal Space
3 Education Lounge
4 Studio Room
5 Performance Space
6 Parking Garage
7 Loading Dock
8 Kitchen Prep
9 Ginkgo Grove

above
A simulcast projection brings events in the opera house free to the public in the garden.

below
Section

opposite
Ground-floor plan

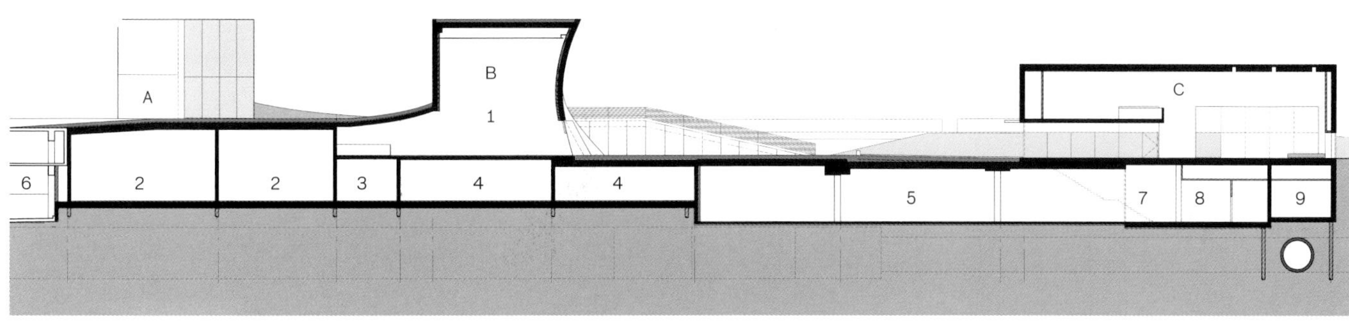

Section 50'

Marking the belowground area, the white concrete structure swoops up from beneath like a glissando in music.

top
Aluminum-formed crinkle concrete merges structure with an acoustical treatment needed for the rehearsal spaces.

right
Topping out, 2018

Comparative Steven Holl Architects Project Sizes

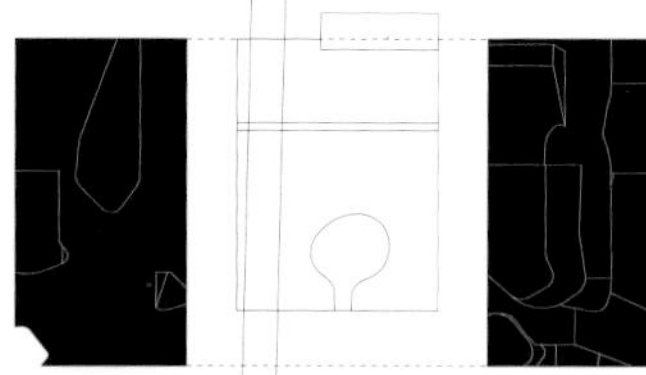

Maggie's Centre
6,500 sf
600 sq m

Hunters Point
24,000 sf
2,200 sq m

VCU, ICA
48,000 sf
4,500 sq m

Doctorate's Building
69,000 sf
6,400 sq m

Alsace
97,000 sf
9,000 sq m

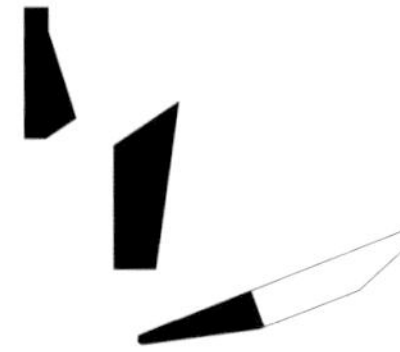

JFK Center Expansion
110,000 sf
10,000 sq m

Reid Building
121,000 sf
11,000 sq m

Visual Arts Building
129,000 sf
12,000 sq m

Lewis Arts Complex
139,000 sf
13,000 sq m

Tianjin Eco-City
581,000 sf
54,000 sq m

Porosity Plan
3,315,000 sf
308,000 sq m

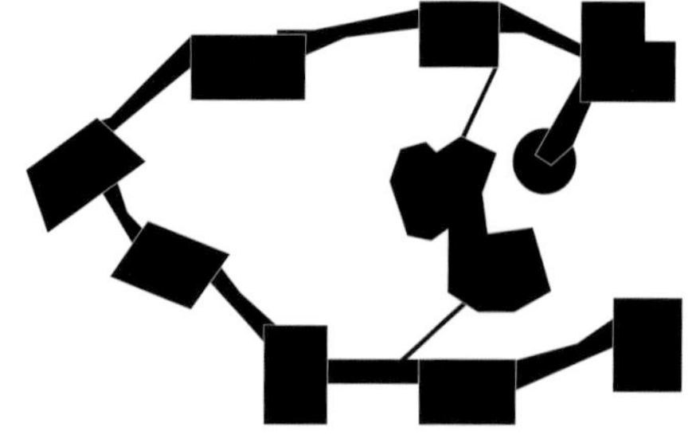

Linked Hybrid
2,383,000 sf
222,000 sq m

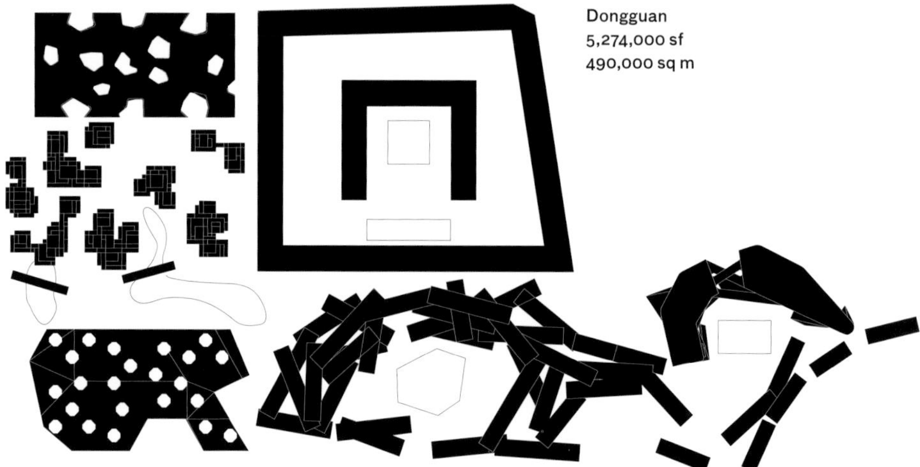

Dongguan
5,274,000 sf
490,000 sq m

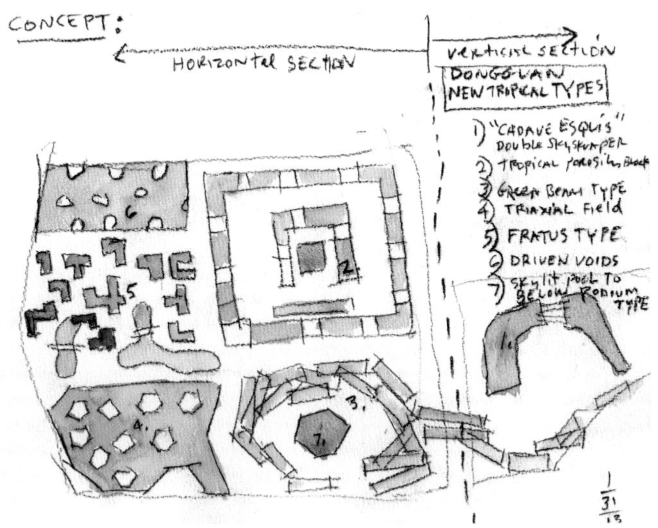

POROSITY PLAN FOR DONGGUAN

Dongguan, China
2012

The client for this commission contacted us with an urgent schedule and a large program that included housing, offices, retail, and recreational and cultural activities. With more than five million square feet (465,000 square meters) of construction, this would provide housing, live/work, and cultural spaces for over 30,000 people (the population of the town I grew up in, Bremerton, Washington).

The plan, a city within a city, is shaped by seven distinct architectural types arranged in a vertical section and a horizontal section. The vertical section comprises two towers based on the exquisite corpse. The horizontal section contains the other six architectural types: Tropical Porosity Block, Green Beams, Triaxial Field, Fractal Towers, Driven Voids, and the Skylit Podium.

The conceptual cement holding the different types together is the lush tropical vegetation of Dongguan's climate. Roofs have a mat system allowing local grasses one meter high to cover all the roofs. This yields a unique view of green from the two towers.

As the overall concept is "heterogeneous tropical porosity," we imagined a reflection on ancient philosopher's stones with their variety of porosity types.

After working five months, we flew to Dongguan to make the presentation in front of a roomful of casually dressed businessmen. Five minutes into the presentation, the oldest man suddenly left the room. A few minutes later, a younger man appeared to announce, "This project is canceled," shocking us.

Architecture is a fragile art and a struggle, but we never give up.

above
For a tropical climate, a great urban density and urban porosity via different building types

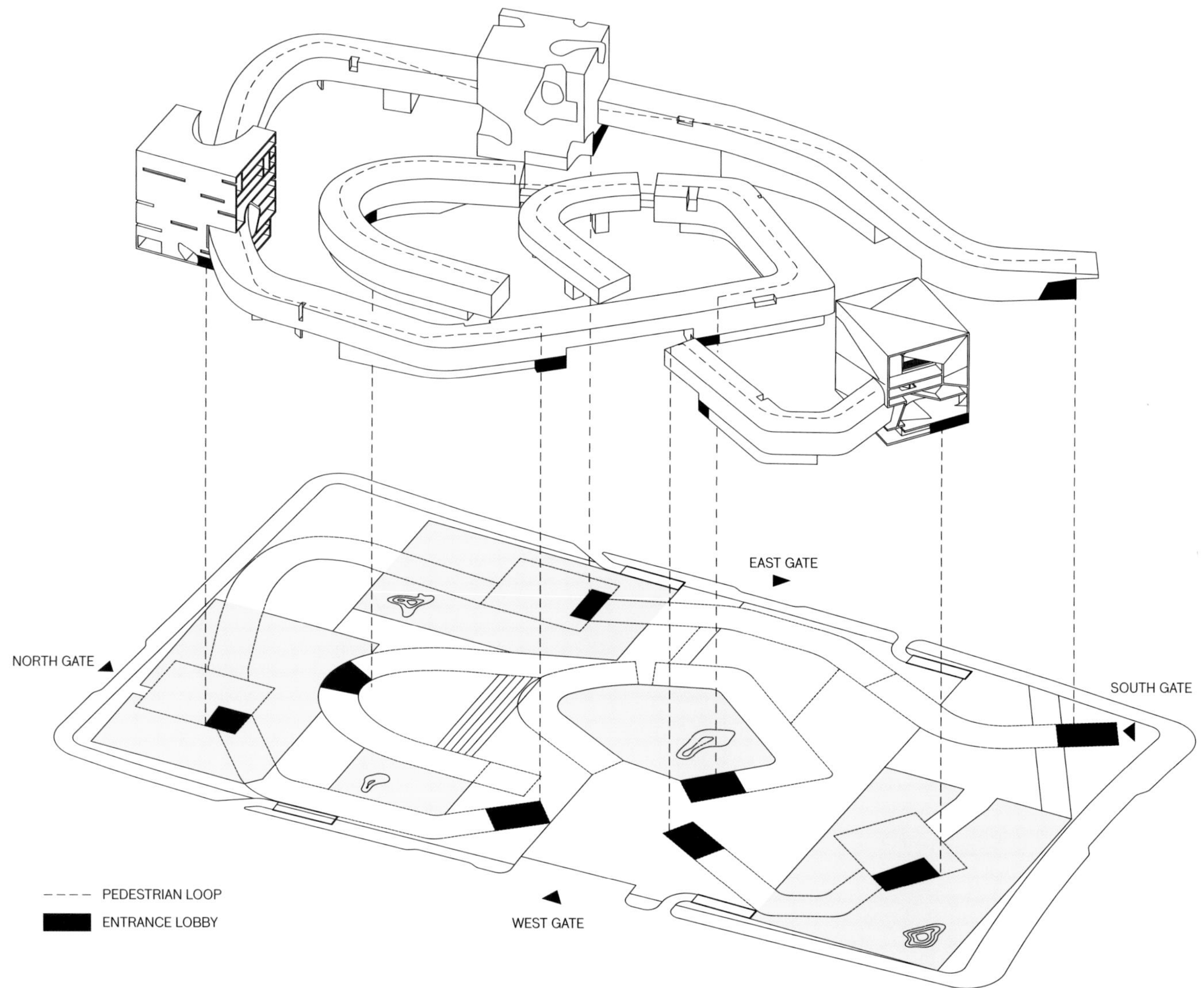

EAST GATE
NORTH GATE
SOUTH GATE
PEDESTRIAN LOOP
ENTRANCE LOBBY
WEST GATE

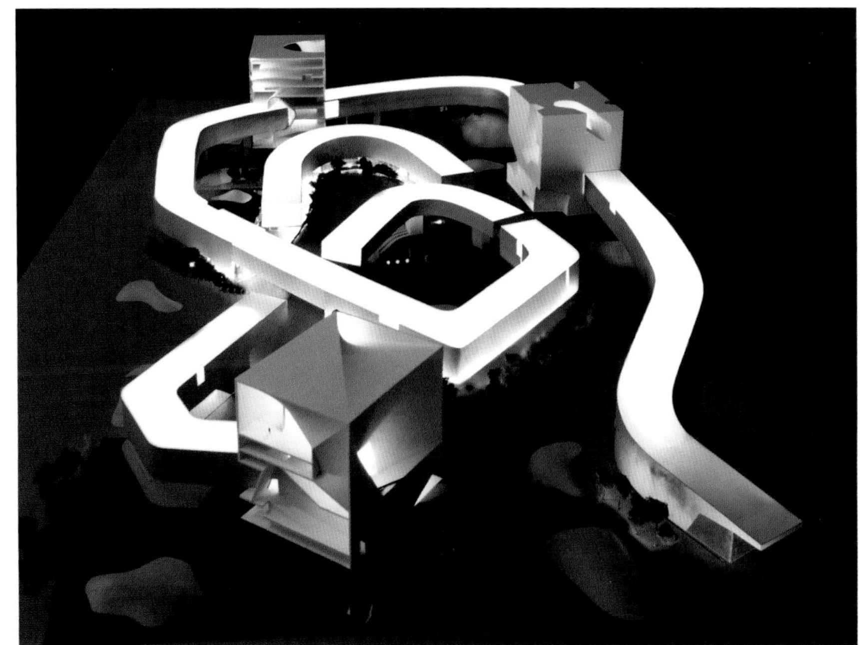

QINGDAO CULTURE AND ART CENTER

Qingdao, China
2013–
Competition: First Place

The linear form of the Jiaozhou Bay Bridge, the world's longest bridge over water, is carried into this project's site in the form of a light loop, which contains gallery spaces and connects all aspects of the landscape and public spaces. The raised light loop allows maximum porosity and movement across the site and permits ocean breezes to flow across the site.

Set within the master plan are art islands, or *yishudao*, which take the form of three sculpted cubes and four small, landscaped art islands that form outdoor sculpture gardens. Five terraced reflecting pools animate the landscape and bring light to levels below via skylights.

The light loop and yishudao concepts facilitate the shaping of public space: a great central square for large gatherings is at the center of the site, overlooking a large water garden.

The new Modern Art Museum shapes the central square. The Public Arts Museum forms the main experience of entry from the south. The North Yishudao contains the Classic Art Museum, with a hotel in its top levels, and the South Yishudao, which floats over the large south reflecting pool, holds the Performing Arts Program.

In the light loop, all horizontal galleries receive natural light from the roof. Light levels can be controlled with modulating 20-percent screens that have blackout options. The 65-foot-wide (20-meter-wide) section of the light loop allows side lighting to enter the lower-level galleries and provides space for two galleries side by side, avoiding dead-end circulation.

The basic architecture is in simple monochrome, composed of sanded marine aluminum and stained concrete, with the undersides of the light loops in the rich polychrome colors of ancient Chinese architecture. These soffits are washed with light at night to become landscape lighting in shimmering reflected colors.

Placed between the skylights on the light loop, photovoltaic cells will fulfill 80 percent of the museum's electrical needs. The reflecting ponds contain recycled water, while 480 geothermal wells provide heating and cooling.

The story of this competition is not yet finished. The site has been cleared, and the project is awaiting government go-ahead.

vimeo.com/78112973

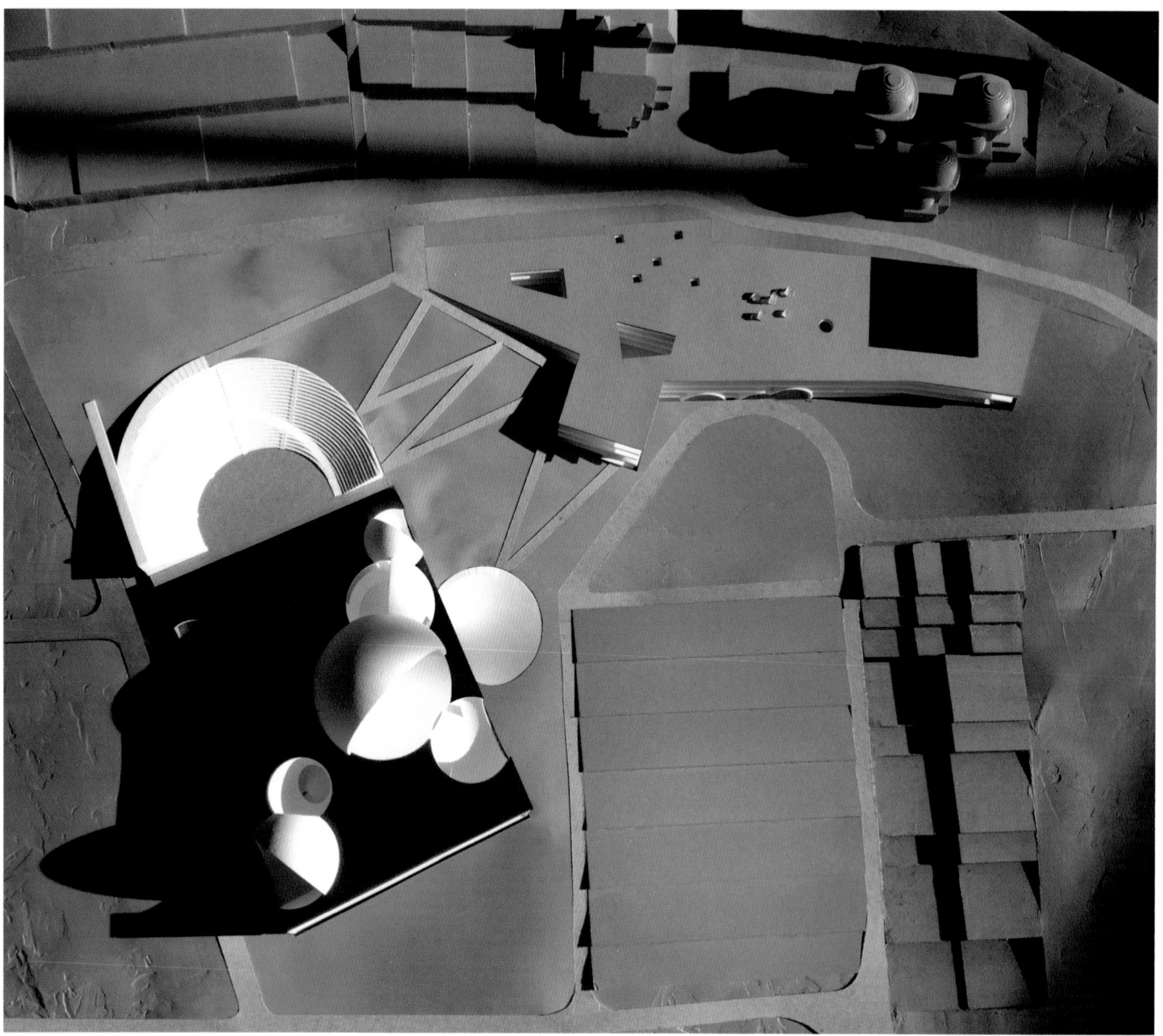

TAIWAN CHINPAOSAN NECROPOLIS

Taipei, Taiwan
2013–

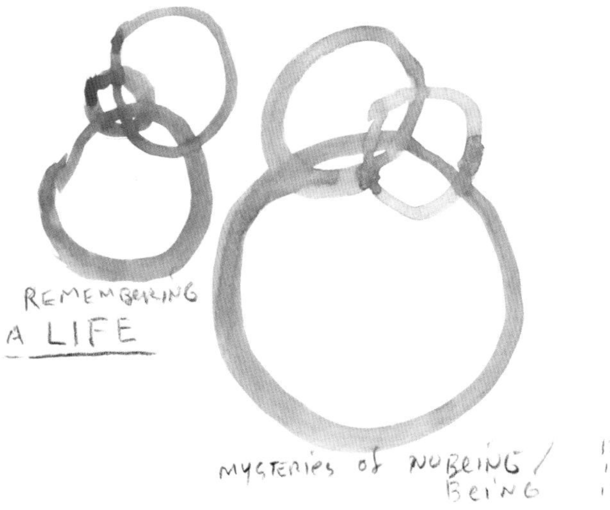

On a magnificent Pacific Ocean site forty minutes from Taipei, the Necropolis of ChinPaoSan requires a new arrival hall and a new pavilion for 150,000 additional ash box sites.

The arrival hall will contain a twenty-one-room hotel, a restaurant, a ceremonial chapel, an auditorium, and two small museums. It takes the shape of the allotted plot, extruded into four levels with spherical subtractions.

The new Oceanic Pavilion will accommodate one thousand people for ceremonial days, as well as fifty presiding Buddhist monks to conduct ceremonies. An adjoining amphitheater will seat five thousand people.

All religions are respected and accommodated in this Necropolis. Its geometry of intersected spheres refers to a rich ancient history. Borromean rings appeared in Buddhist art, Viking rune stones, and Roman mosaics thousands of years ago. Borromean rings also represent the karmic laws of the universe and the interconnectedness of life. The intersecting spheres are embedded in a rectangular plan topped by a sheet of water, pulling the ocean's horizon into the composition.

Photovoltaic cells sit inches below this water sheet, providing 60 percent of the electricity for both buildings. Cooling via the water increases the photovoltaic efficiency by 20 percent. Natural light is brought into the building section through openings in the intersecting spheres.

Urn shelving, which occupies most of the building's section, is arranged in different typologies: radial, circular, and orthogonal. The Oceanic Pavilion is composed of white concrete with granite floors. Hinoki wood is used for doors and partitions. Ceremonial areas are treated in translucent alabaster and gold leaf.

above
Concept sketch, 2013

opposite
Water-roofed Oceanic Pavilion and Arrival Hall with green roofs

Site plan 200m

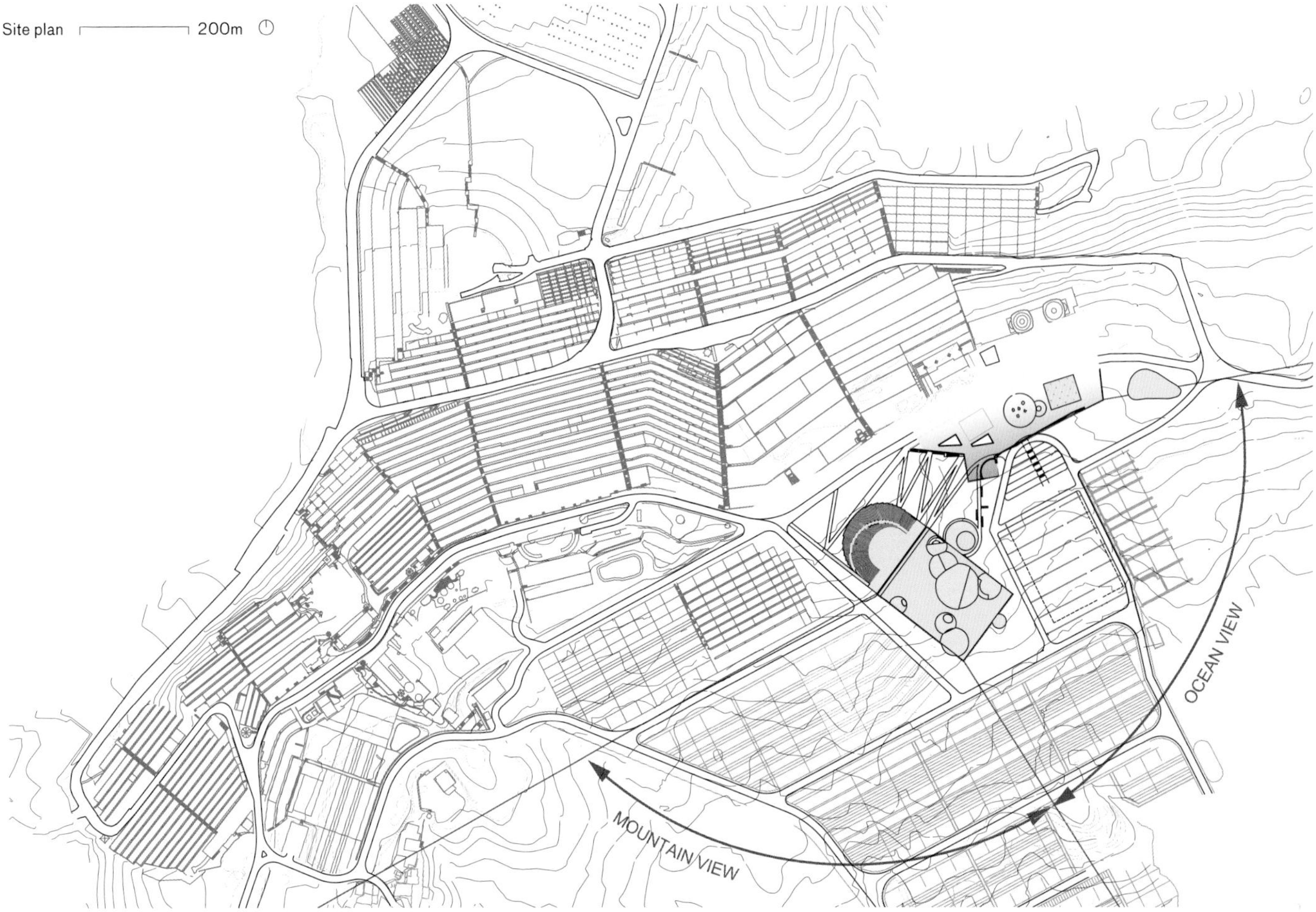

OCEAN VIEW

MOUNTAIN VIEW

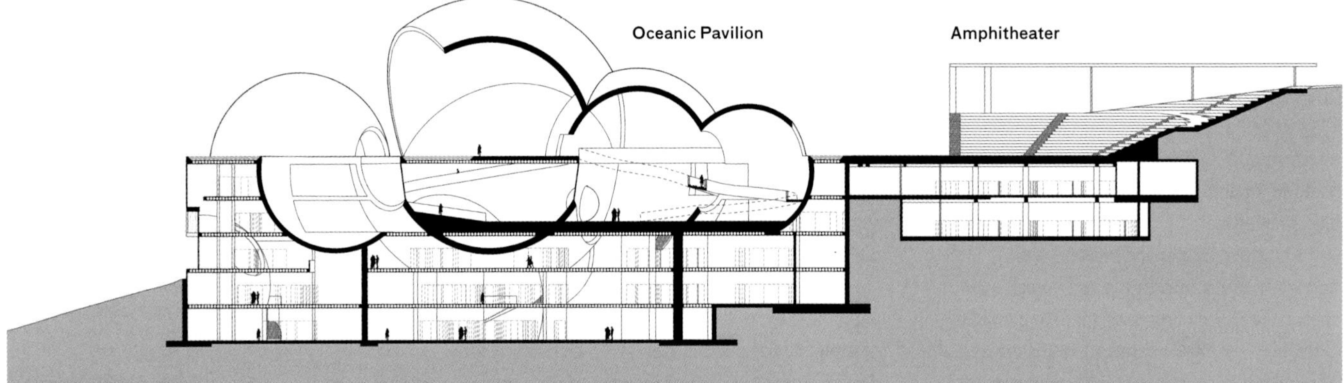

Section 25m

opposite
The Necropolis of ChinPaoSan near Taipei already has over ten thousand burial sites. The new Arrival Hall and Oceanic Pavilion are centrally located on the hillside with Pacific Ocean views.

top left
Three times a year, events draw over one thousand people and hundreds of Buddhist monks.

top right
Model study of Arrival Hall showing dynamic spatial energy via intersecting spheres

right
Construction: a hybrid of steel encased in white concrete

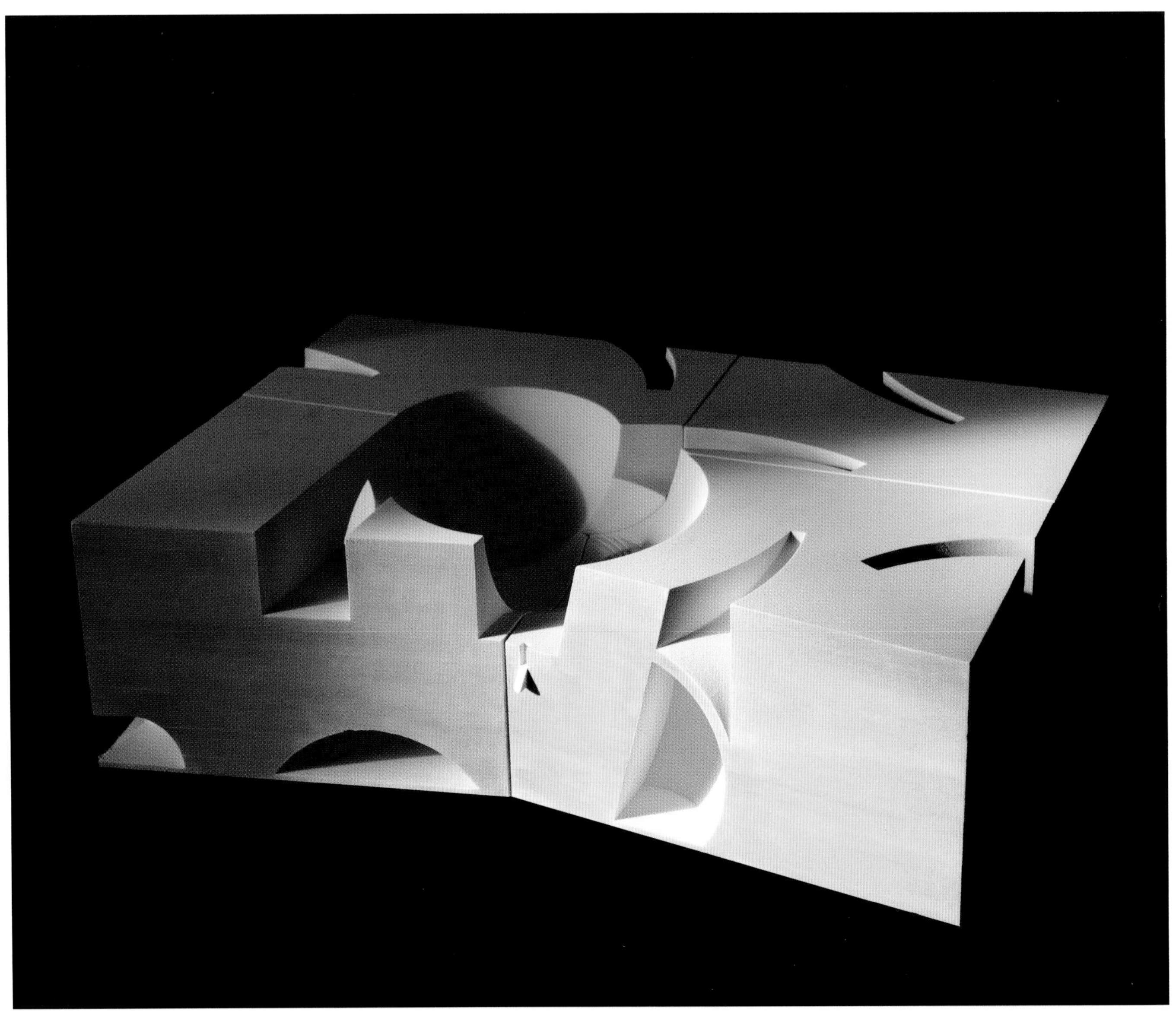

Sculpted, diffused light via subtractive cuts

MUMBAI CITY MUSEUM NORTH WING

Mumbai, India
2014–15
Competition: First Place

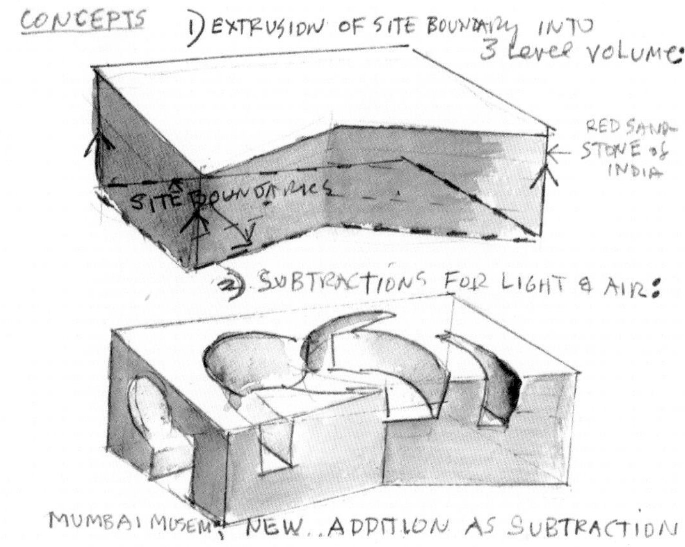

The Mumbai City Museum's North Wing addition is envisioned as a sculpted subtraction from a simple geometry formed by the site boundaries. The concept of "addition as subtraction" is developed in stained concrete with sculpted, diffused light in the new 65,000-square-foot (6,039-square-meter) gallery spaces. Deeper subtractive cuts bring in twenty-five foot-candles of natural light to each gallery at eye level.

The light cuts provide the orthogonal galleries with a sense of flow and spatial overlap. The central cut forms a shaded monsoon water basin that runs into a central pool, reminiscent of the great stepped well architecture of India. The central pool joins the new and old in its reflection and provides 60 percent of the museum's electricity through photovoltaic cells located below the water's surface.

On December 6, 2014, our partner Noah Yaffe was in Mumbai, but I could not fly there to present the design, so the jury allowed me to join via Skype at 10:00 p.m. At 4:30 a.m. I received a text: "We won!" It was so immediate, yet now years have passed due to city political delays. The story of this international competition continues as we wait for Mumbai's 2019 elections.

Upper-level gallery: a continuous circulation flow through orthogonal galleries with natural light

Cooling Basin above central pool. Rain will be a visual event in this public space.

Upper-level floor plan 20m

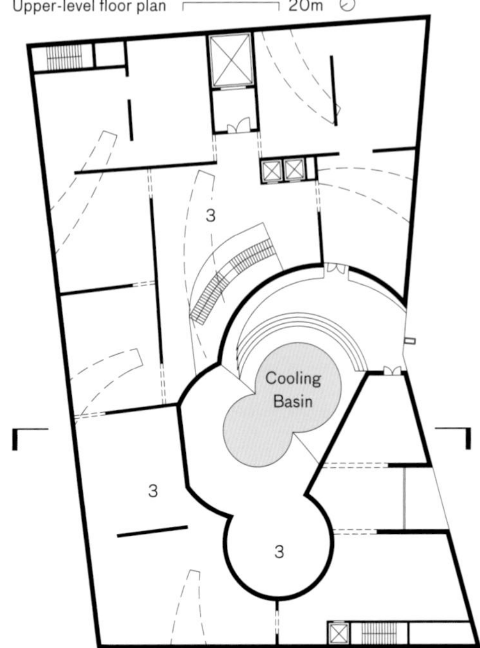

1 Entry
2 Foyer
3 Gallery
4 Reception
5 Garden
6 Restaurant/Cafe
7 Shop
8 Staff & Offices
9 Conference Center
10 Garden Courtyard
11 Reflecting Pond
12 Artists' Workshop and Residence
13 Staff Entry
14 Conservation Lab
15 Connecting Tunnel
16 Parking

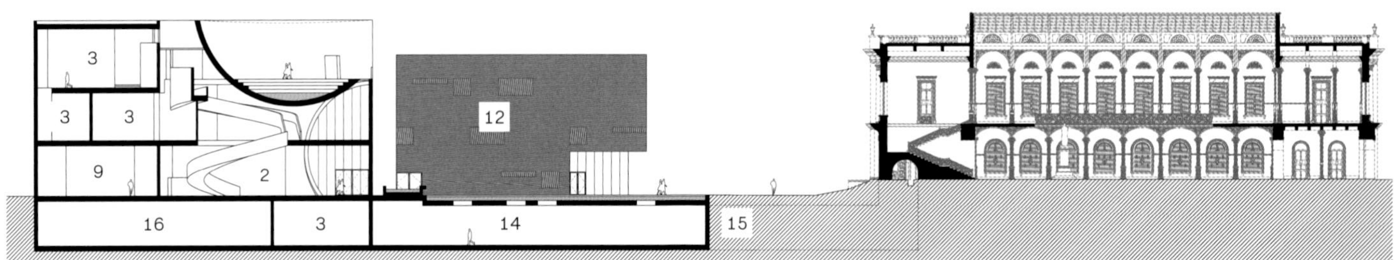

Section 20m

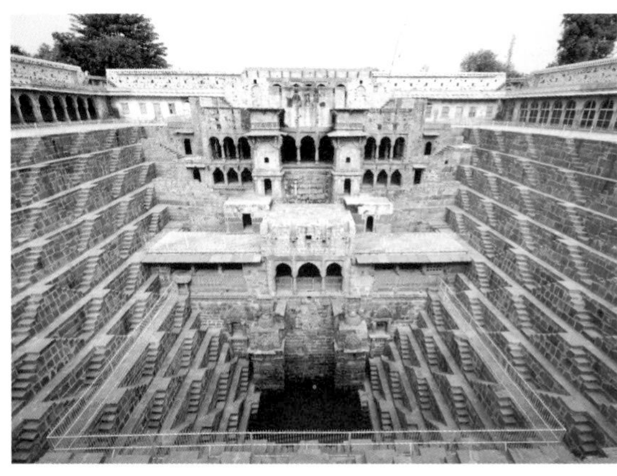

The subtractive architecture of the step wells of India cuts deep into the earth for year-round water access. The wells date from 200 CE. Today India has 1.3 billion people, one billion more than the United States. The public education provided by a museum can be a gift to the future.

Ground-floor plan 20m

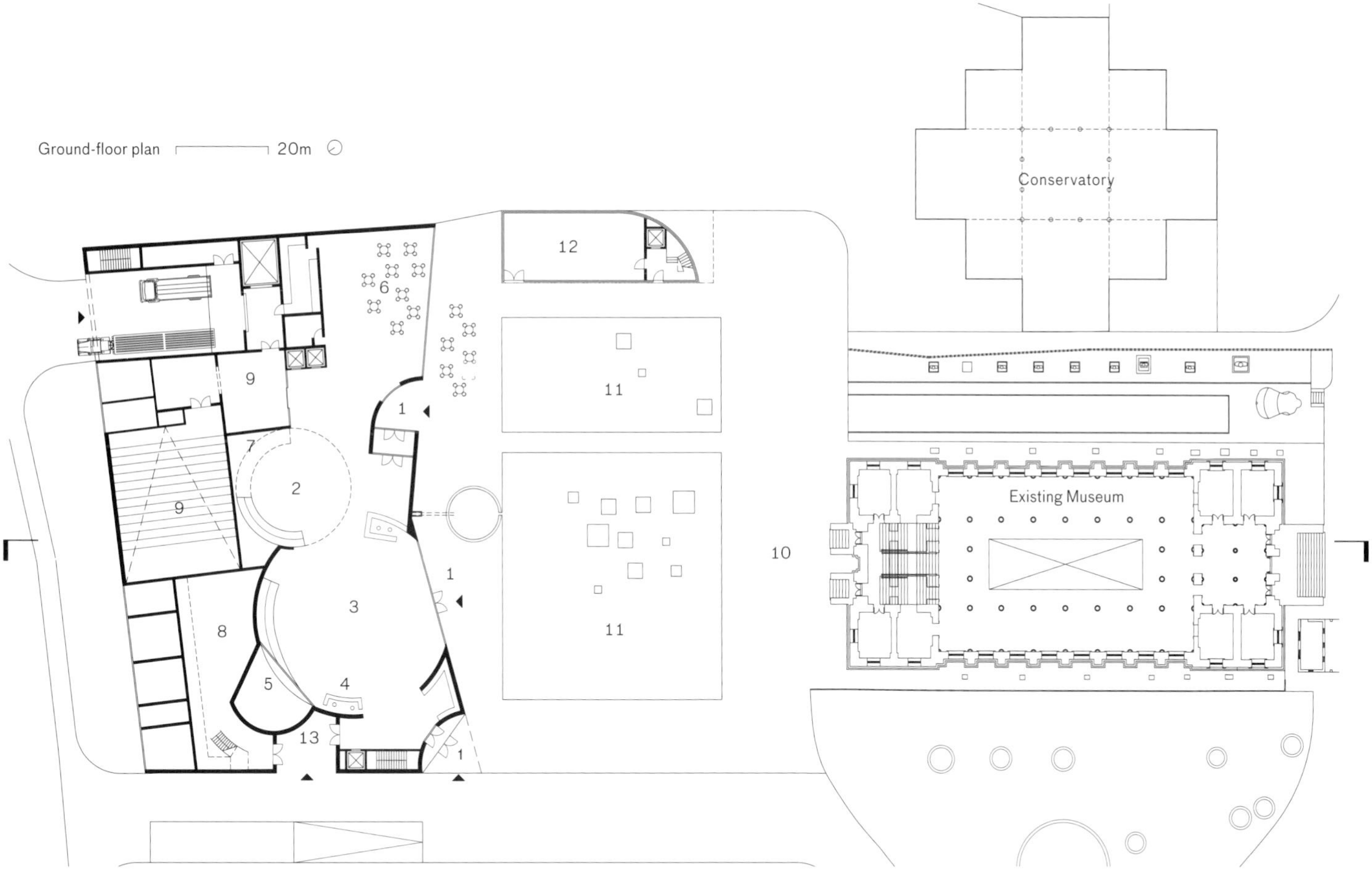

Conservatory
Existing Museum
1
2
3
4
5
6
7
8
9
10
11
12
13

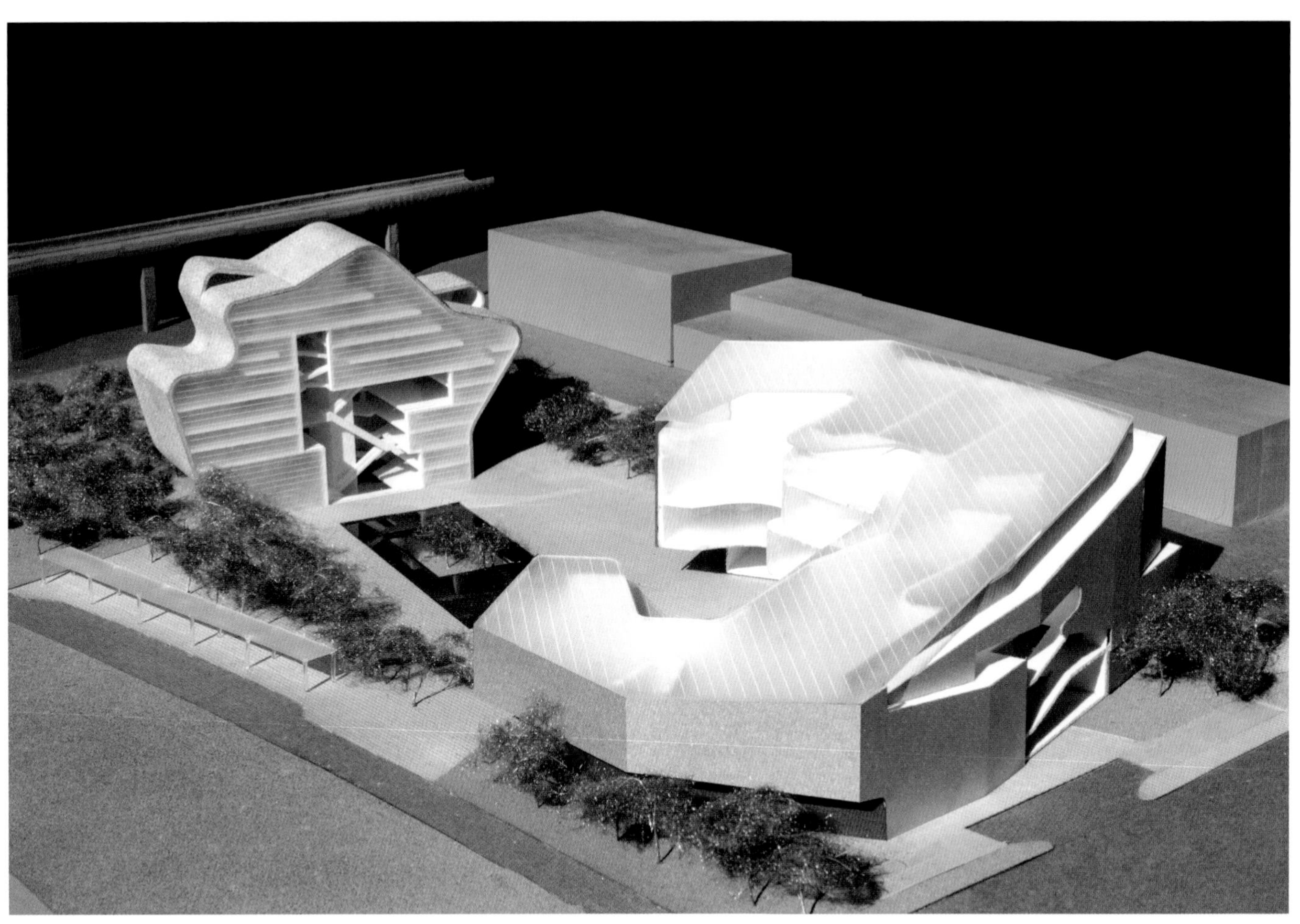

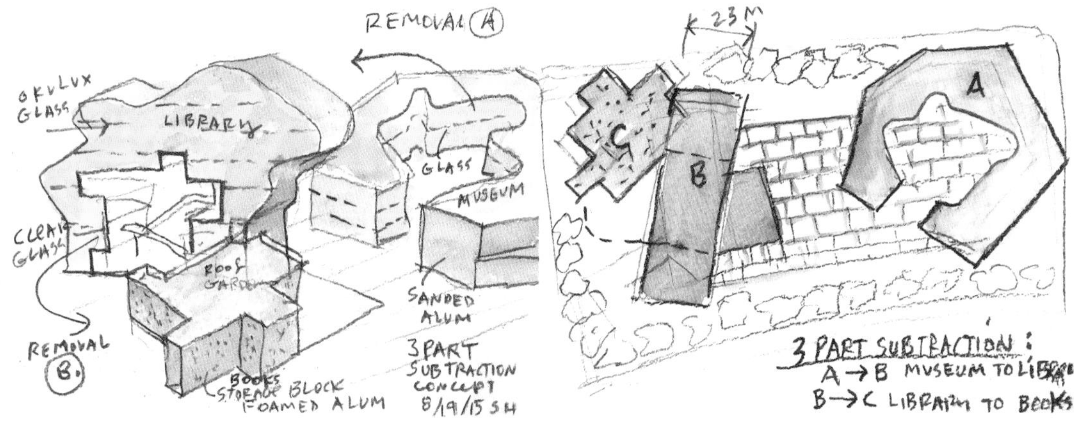

SHENZHEN LIBRARY AND ART MUSEUM

Shenzhen, China
2015

This design competition was for a new public library and museum on a site in a developing section of Shenzhen. Rectangular condominium towers already surround the site, which is next to a tram stop.

Our aim was to shape public space with two buildings connected below the plaza level.

The massing concept is a three-part removal. The optimal museum typology for light and circulation is horizontal. From this horizontal mass, we subtracted the volume of the library, forming a central courtyard for the museum and a figural shape for the library.

Subtracted from the central body of the library, the mechanical book block leaves a clear glass void cut, marking double front entrances facing east and west.

Solar photovoltaic cells on the museum's roof tilt at an optimal angle facing due south, collecting 90 percent of the energy needed to operate the buildings. As the solar photovoltaic cells and their spacing are translucent, the entire top-floor galleries of the museum receive a soft, filtered natural light.

The museum and library's roof rainwater is collected in the recycled water of the plaza's pools and is recirculated in the pools' fountains. Geothermal cooling and radiant floors bring the entire complex a LEED Platinum rating.

The material of the museum is sanded marine aluminum with clear and Okalux glass, providing soft light and only 18 percent light transmission. The book block T is of foamed aluminum.

Our design received the most votes from the jury; however, city officials chose a different scheme, overriding the jury. At the time of this writing, the project remains unbuilt.

vimeo.com/328424153

above
Concept sketch, 2015

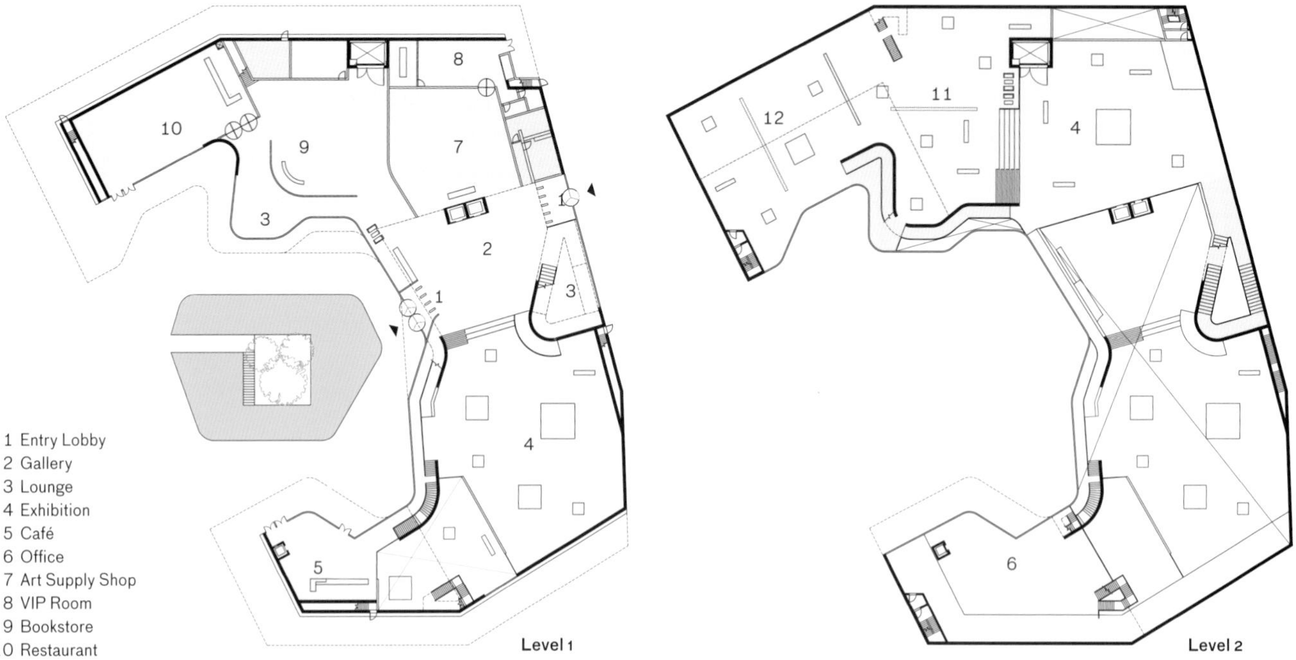

Level 1

Level 2

1 Entry Lobby
2 Gallery
3 Lounge
4 Exhibition
5 Café
6 Office
7 Art Supply Shop
8 VIP Room
9 Bookstore
10 Restaurant
11 Small Exhibition
12 Sculpture Exhibition

Museum floor plans 100'

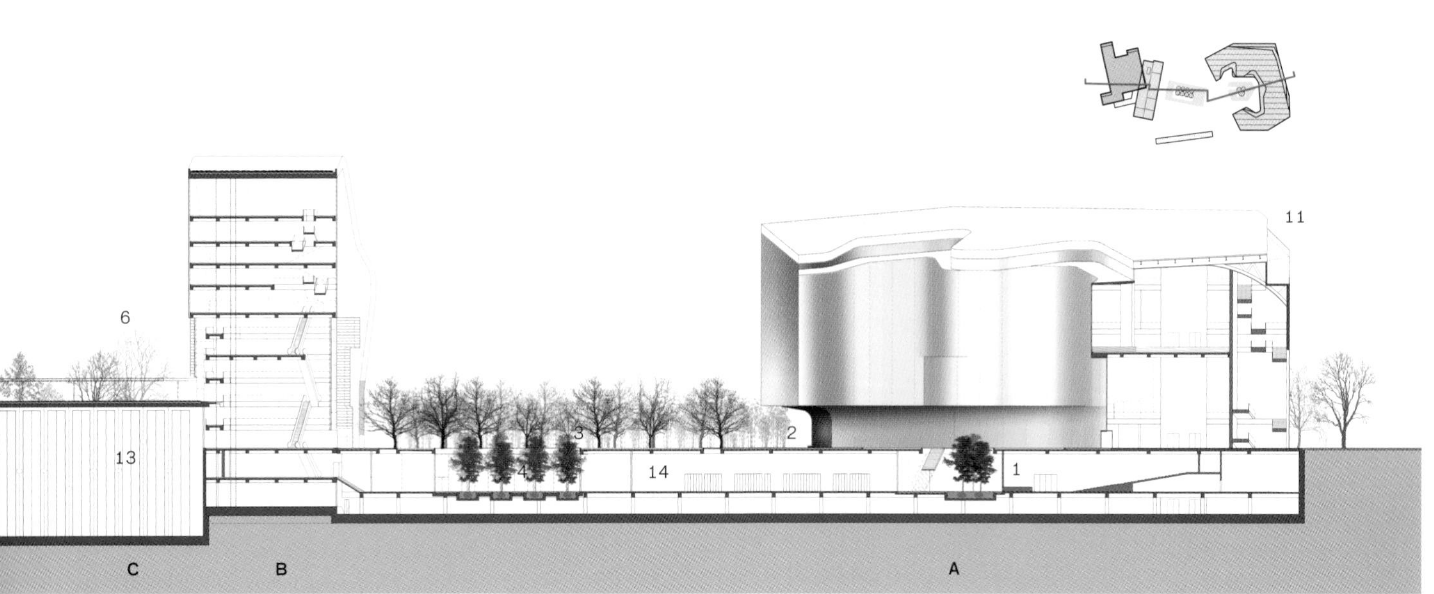

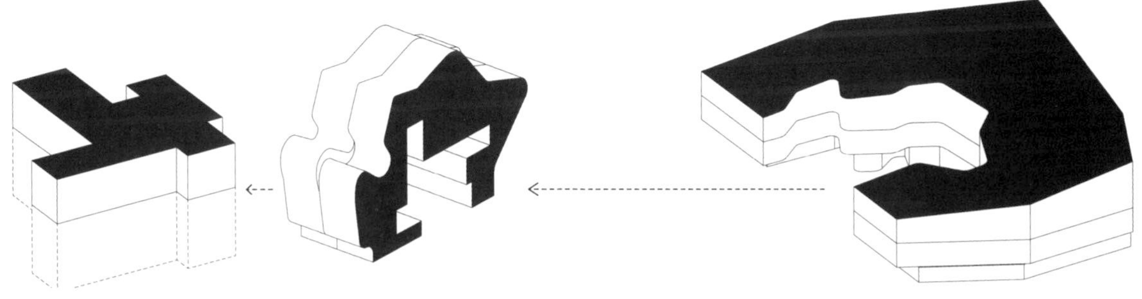

Intelligent Book Stack | Library | Museum

below and
opposite, bottom

- A Art Museum
- B Library
- C Book Stack

1. Auditorium / Sunken Garden
2. Waterlily Pond
3. Reflecting Pool & Fountain
4. Children's Library / Sunken Garden
5. Sculpture Plaza
6. Reading Garden
7. Glass Awning
8. Drop-off
9. Bike Parking
10. Bus Parking
11. Car Parking
12. Skypath
13. Library Retrieval System
14. Compact Stacks

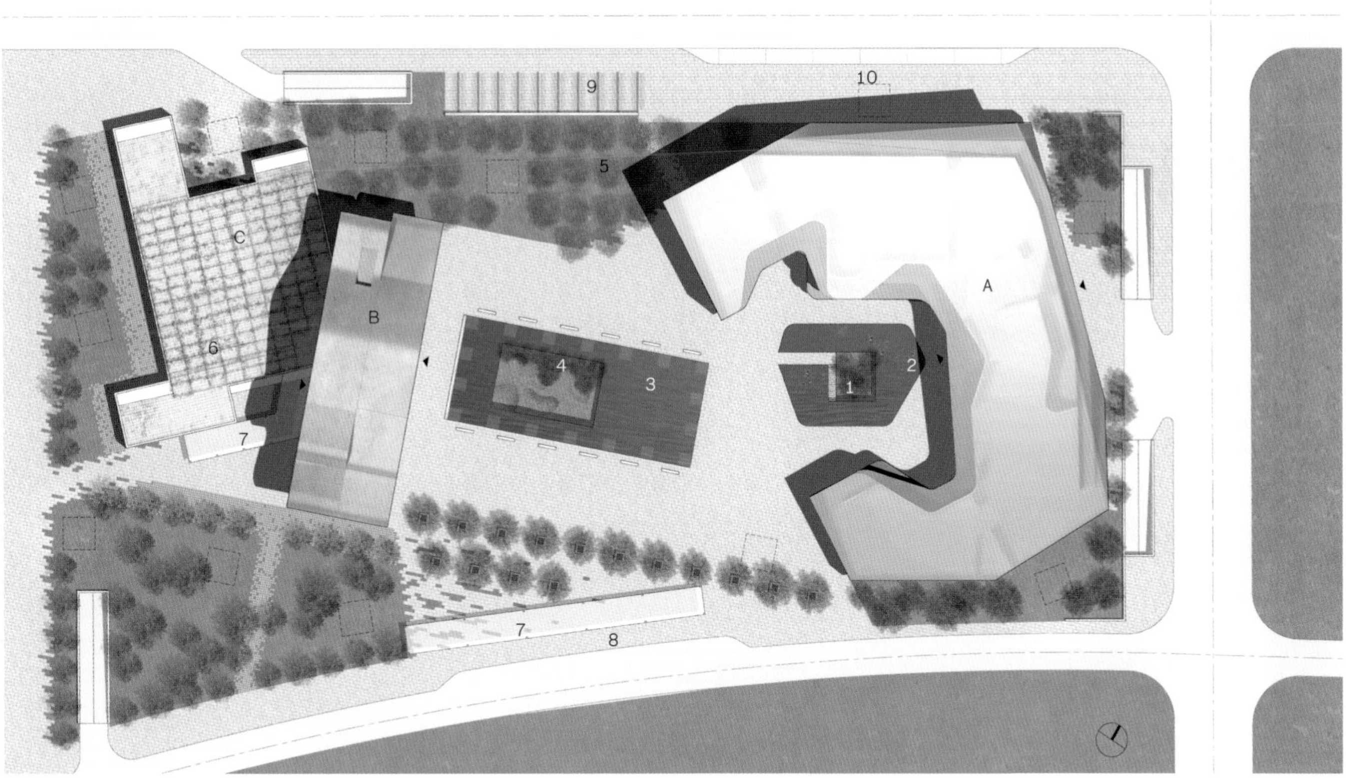

RUBENSTEIN COMMONS INSTITUTE FOR ADVANCED STUDY

Princeton, New Jersey, USA

2015–19

Competition: First Place

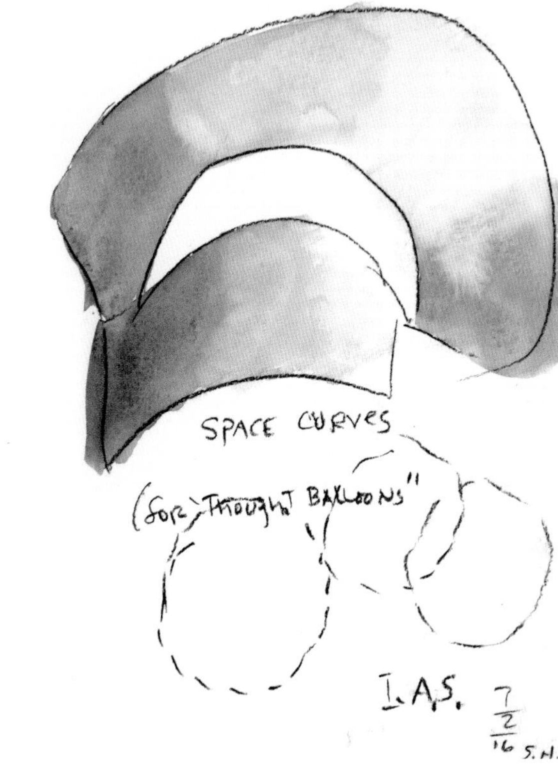

The Institute for Advanced Study in Princeton, established in 1930, is adding a new commons building near its original 1939 building, Fuld Hall, where Albert Einstein spent his last working years.

The new Rubenstein Commons Building will be a social condenser, providing campus scholars a place of inspiration and provoking conversation and interaction. It will contain several meeting rooms of different sizes, a restaurant and outdoor café, a living room, a gallery of campus history, and several offices.

The building intertwines with the landscape, connecting with pools of water in all four directions. The pools reflect sunlight into interior spaces, producing an atmosphere of reflection. Natural phenomena are interwoven with science, physics, humanities, and art, corresponding with the institute's mission.

The geometry of the spaces is formed by space curves where two nonplanar curves intersect. The director of the IAS remarked that the curved ceilings provide room for the thought bubbles of the scholars. Prismatic glass breaks white light into the color spectrum, energizing the interior.

The curved roofs are in verdigris weathered copper—the same as the roofs of Fuld Hall and other campus buildings. The bent-pipe steel structure is supported on precast concrete walls.

The building is geothermally heated and cooled and naturally ventilated.

above
Competition concept sketch, 2016

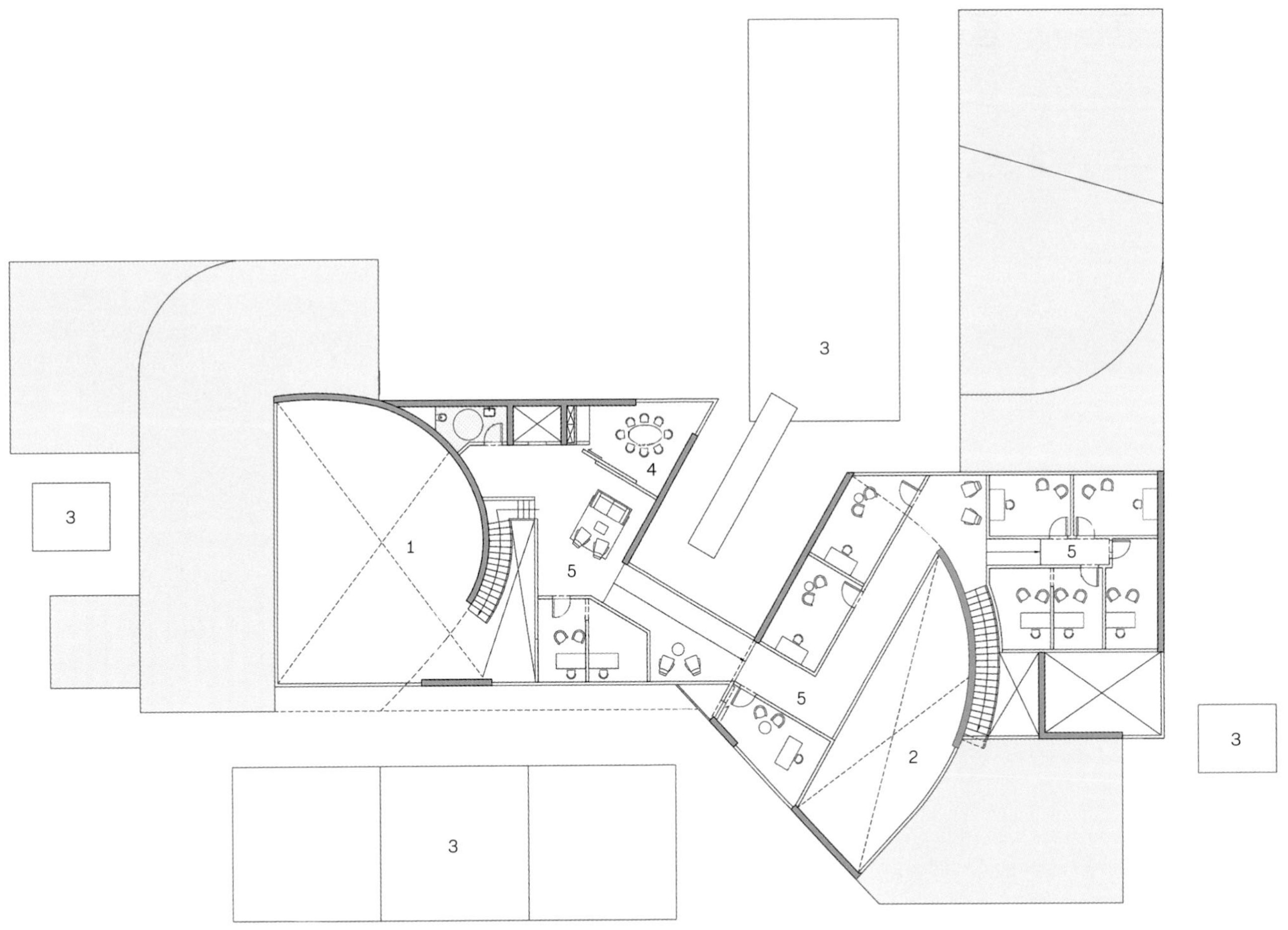

1 Café
2 Living Room
3 Pool
4 Meeting Room
5 Office

Mezzanine floor plan 20'

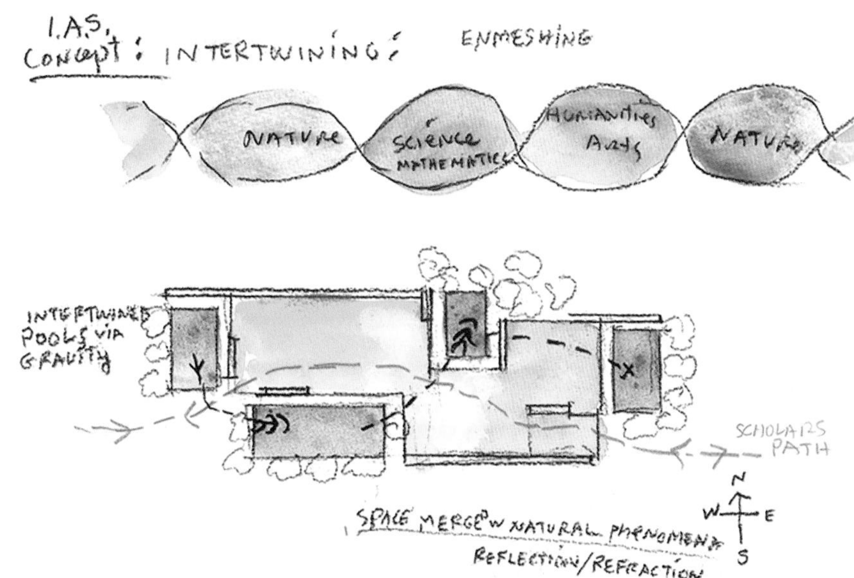

Culture must be one of the foundations for world understanding.
—ALBERT EINSTEIN
UNESCO COURIER, DECEMBER 1951

above
Getting approval from the authorities

top right
Concept watercolor: intertwining

right
Construction, 2018

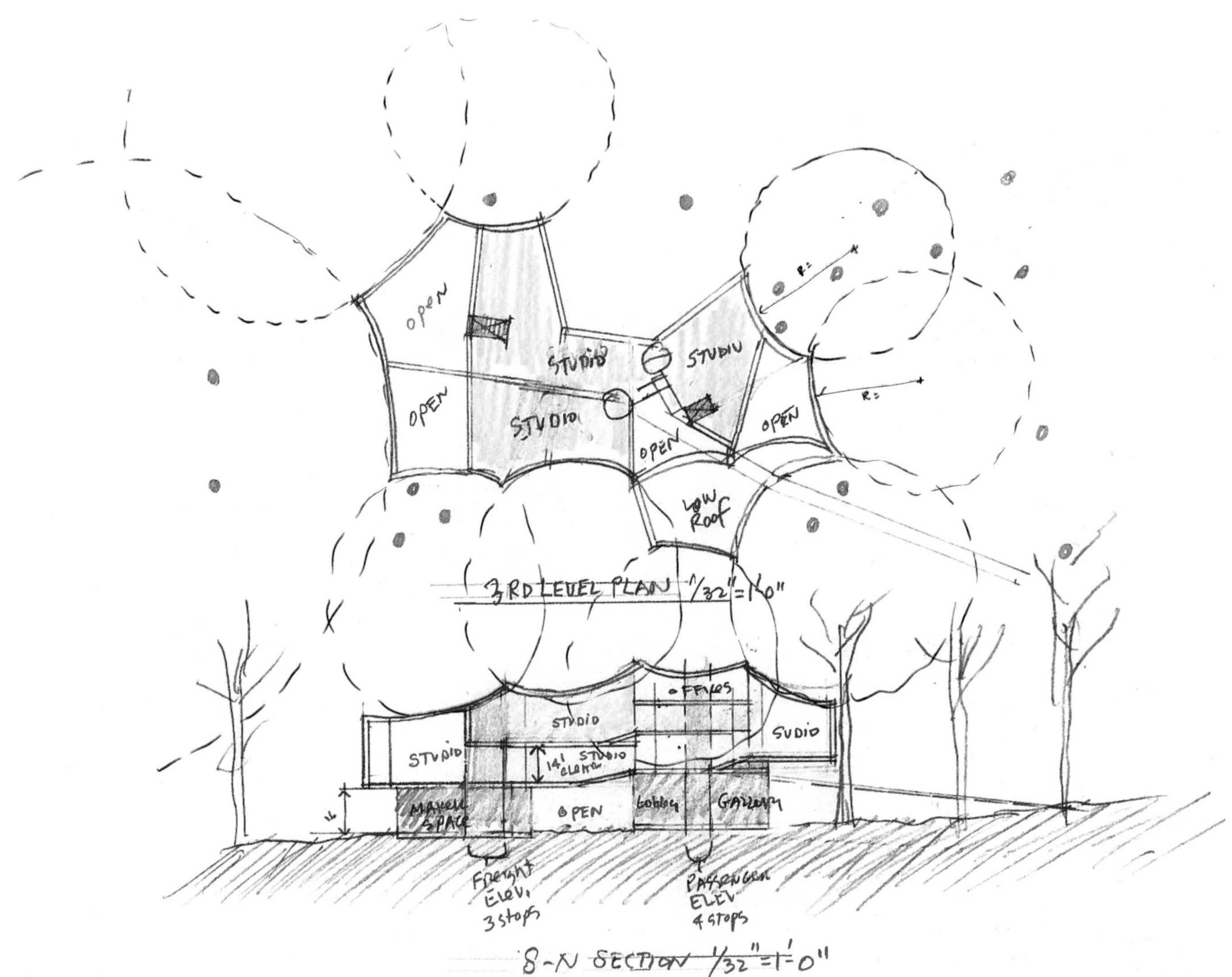
open
OPEN
STUDIO
STUDIO
STUDIO
OPEN
OPEN
LOW Roof
3RD LEVEL PLAN 1/32" = 1'-0"
OFFICES
STUDIO
SUDIO
STUDIO
14' STUDIO
OPEN
LOBBY
GALLERY
FREIGHT ELEV. 3 stops
PASSENGER ELEV 4 stops
S-N SECTION 1/32" = 1'-0"

WINTER VISUAL ARTS CENTER FRANKLIN & MARSHALL COLLEGE

Lancaster, Pennsylvania, USA
2016–19

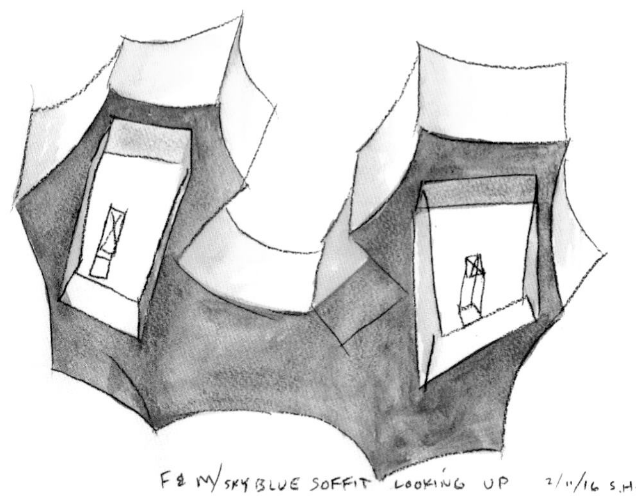

A first reflection on the new Winter Visual Arts Center for Franklin & Marshall College led me to remember Benjamin Franklin's kite on that rainy and thunderstruck night when he first harnessed electricity—a story every American child hears while growing up. My initial sketches of a building like a kite stuck in the trees were a playful start.

The college's fifty-two-acre campus is an arboretum of more than one thousand trees. On further study, we realized that these great trees are the oldest and most prominent geometric force characterizing this special place. We thought of the geometry of trees as a way to give shape to the new arts building. Instead of echoing the rectangular block of the existing arts building, the new pavilion would take its shape from the inflection of the diameters of those large campus trees. The kite-in-the-trees sketch now had a much stronger conceptual grounding in the specifics of the site.

Ben Winter, the main donor, and college president Daniel Porterfield both leaned forward at the presentation, exclaiming: "This is a brilliant idea!" Great clients are the essential ingredient in realizing architecture.

opposite
Concave geometry in the initial concept sketch, based on the diameter of the big existing trees, the oldest elements of the campus

1 Commons
2 Gallery
3 Printmaking Studio
4 Painting Studio
5 Design Studio
6 Woodworking Shop
7 Drawing Studio
8 Storage Room
9 Cinema
10 Office
11 Kitchen

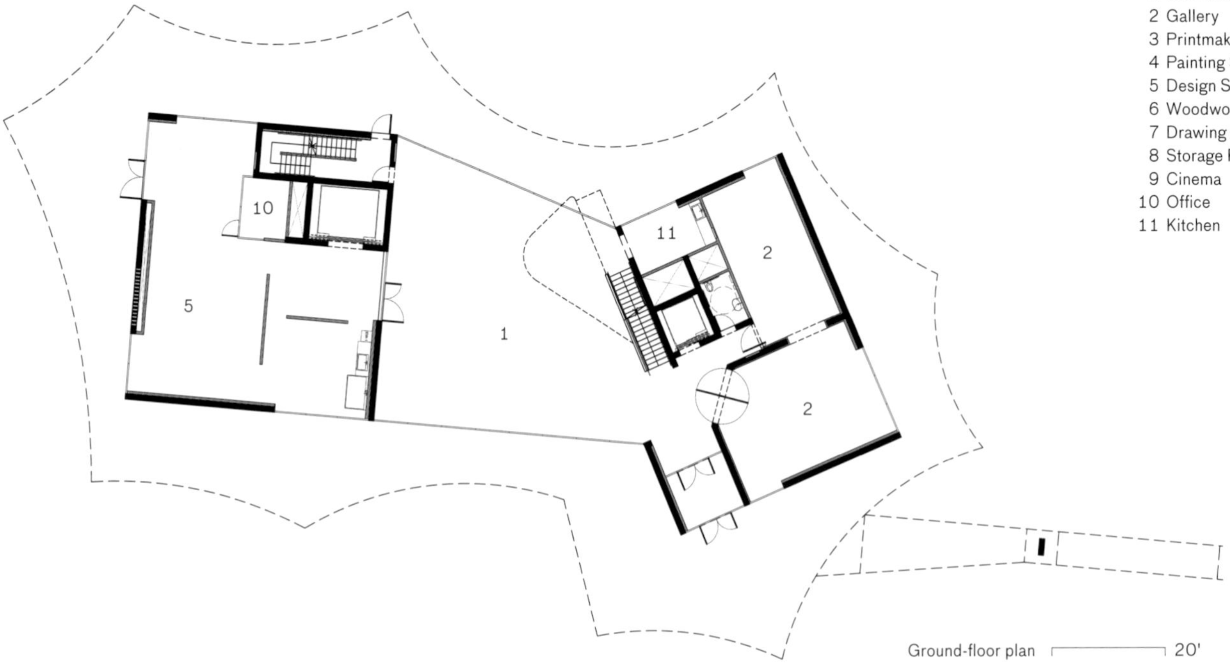

Ground-floor plan 20'

A stormwater retaining pool provides a reflective focus in the new arts quad. A connection to Buchanan Park to the north is made through the ground-level glass forum.

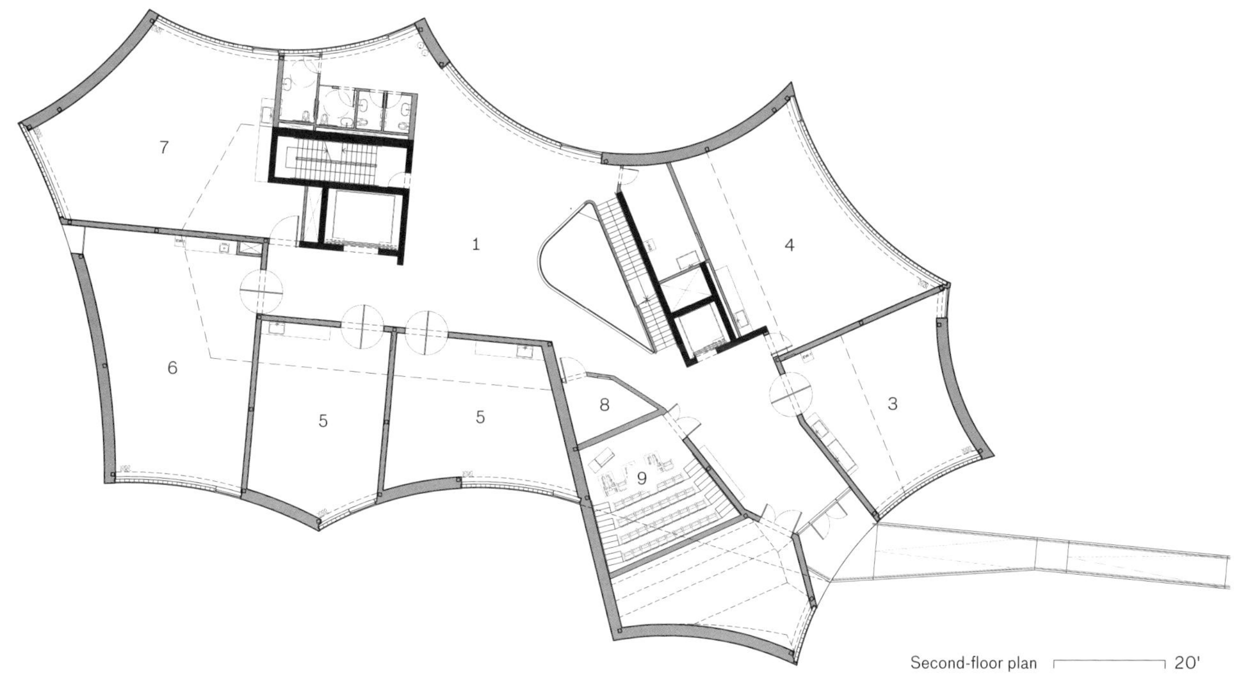

Second-floor plan 20'

below, left
All studios have cool, natural light as well as operable windows. Floors in terrazzo ground concrete provide radiant heat.

below, right
Under construction, 2018

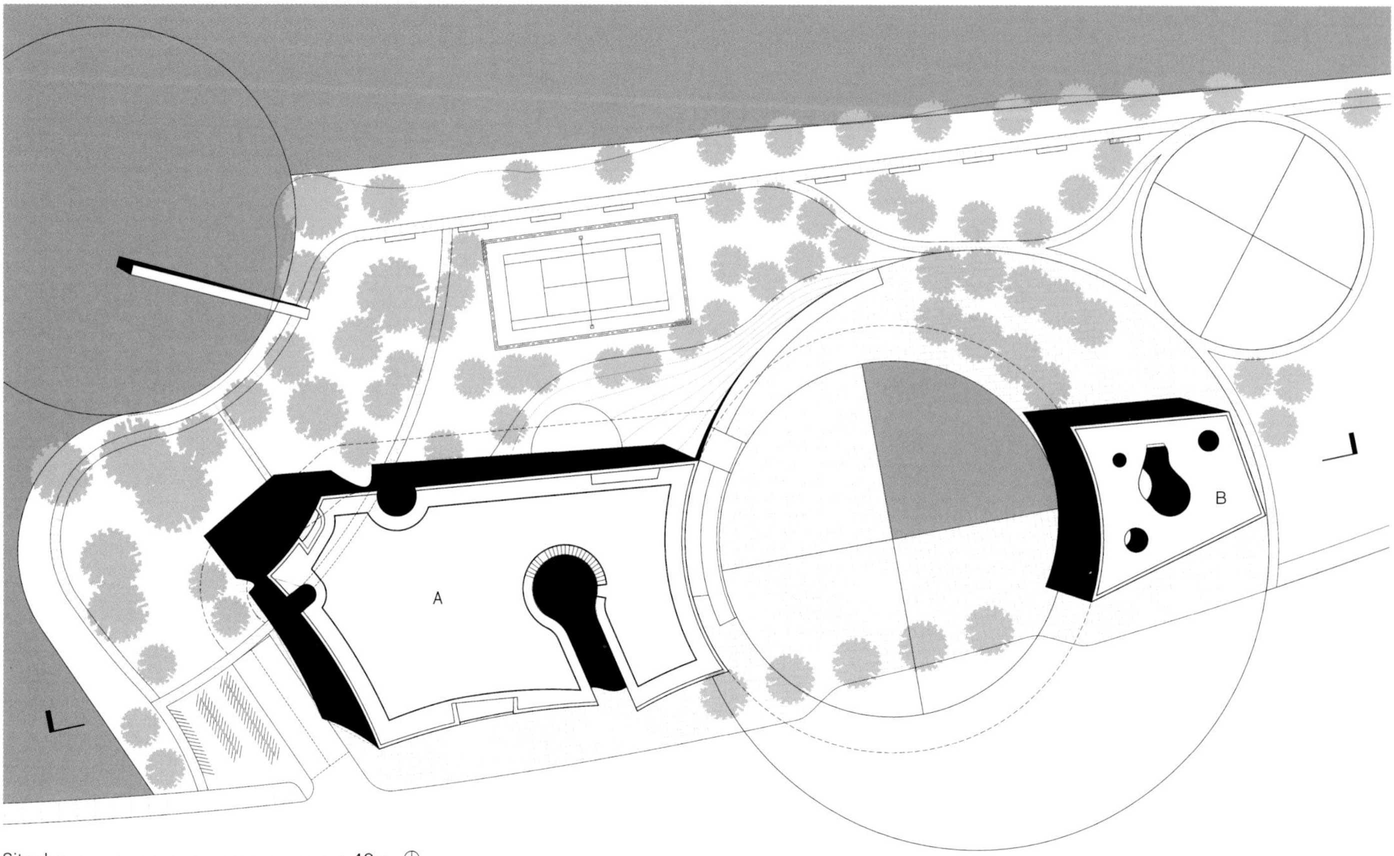

Site plan 40m

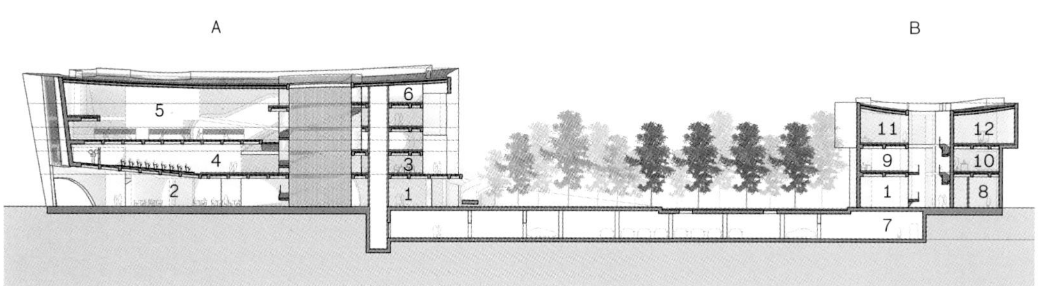

A Cultural Center
B Health Center

1 Reception
2 Leisure Area/Table Games
3 Internet Service
4 Auditorium
5 Badminton
6 Group Activities
7 Service
8 Health Hut
9 Treatment Room
10 ECG & Office
11 Transfusion Room
12 Archive

Site section 40m

COFCO CULTURAL AND HEALTH CENTER

Shanghai, China
2016–

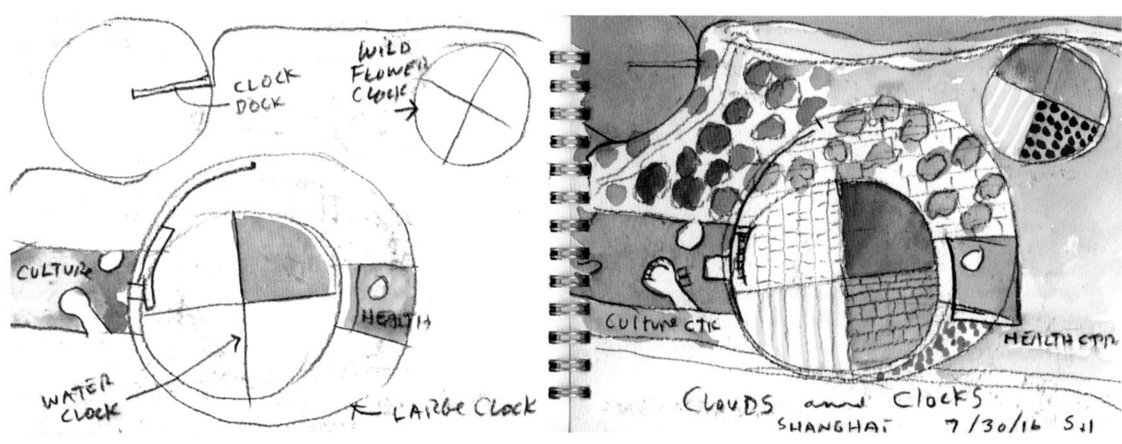

The new Shanghai Cofco Cultural and Health Center aims at being a social condenser, fostering community among the residents of the surrounding new housing blocks with a public space and park along an existing canal. While the housing blocks are repetitive and extensive, here the architecture is of spatial energy and openness, inviting the whole community in for recreational and cultural programs.

The landscape and two new public buildings are merged by the concept of clocks and clouds. The landscape is organized in large, clocklike circles forming a central public space, and the buildings are cloudlike in their porosity and openness. The Cultural Center, built out of white concrete, hovers over a transparent glass base that exposes a café and game and recreation rooms. A curved ramp, climbing gently up to the second floor, creates a continuous experience of overlooking.

The Health Center, also made of white concrete, is shaped by the curves of the landscape, developing a strong relationship among its cloudlike parts. Both buildings have green sedum roofs, which merges them further with the landscape when seen from the surrounding apartment buildings above.

A quarter-circle pool and fountain reflect the building's central space and provide rainwater recycling. The buildings, which are geothermally cooled, aim to be LEED Platinum.

left
At the heart of the Cultural Center is an opening to the sky with mysterious light.

above
Clouds model. The white concrete structure with strategic openings for interior light will form the facade.

below
The Health Center faces the Cultural Center, forming a curved public space.

Detail of model shows the main entry of the Cultural Center.

in his lecture “Of Clouds and Clocks,” Karl Popper (1902–1994) formulated an evolutionary model of free will.

1 Entry
2 Exhibition
3 Lounge
4 Café
5 Activity Area
6 Table Game Area
7 Pharmacy
8 Health Hut
9 Health Inquiry
10 Registration
11 Civic Plaza
12 Pond

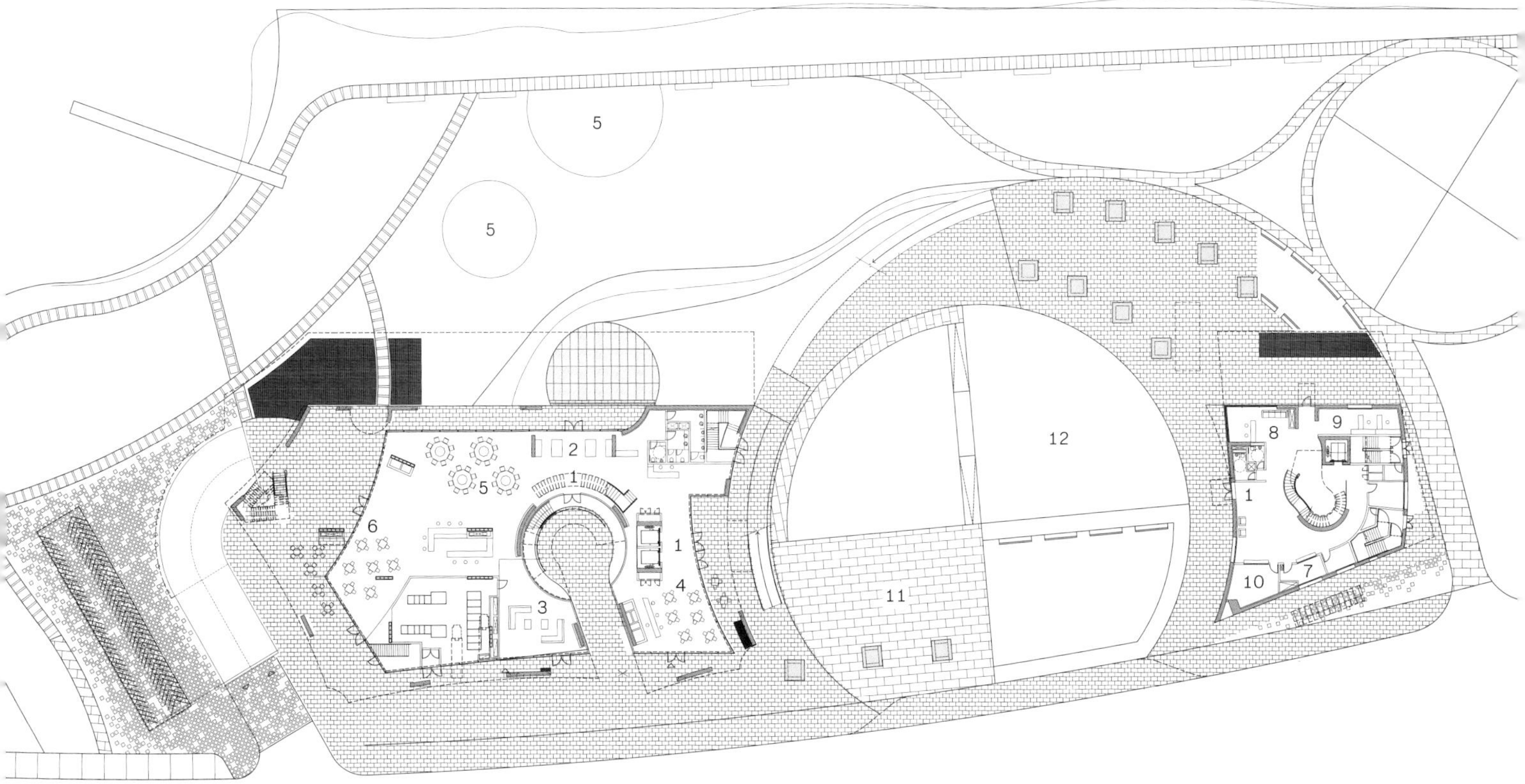

Site plan 20m

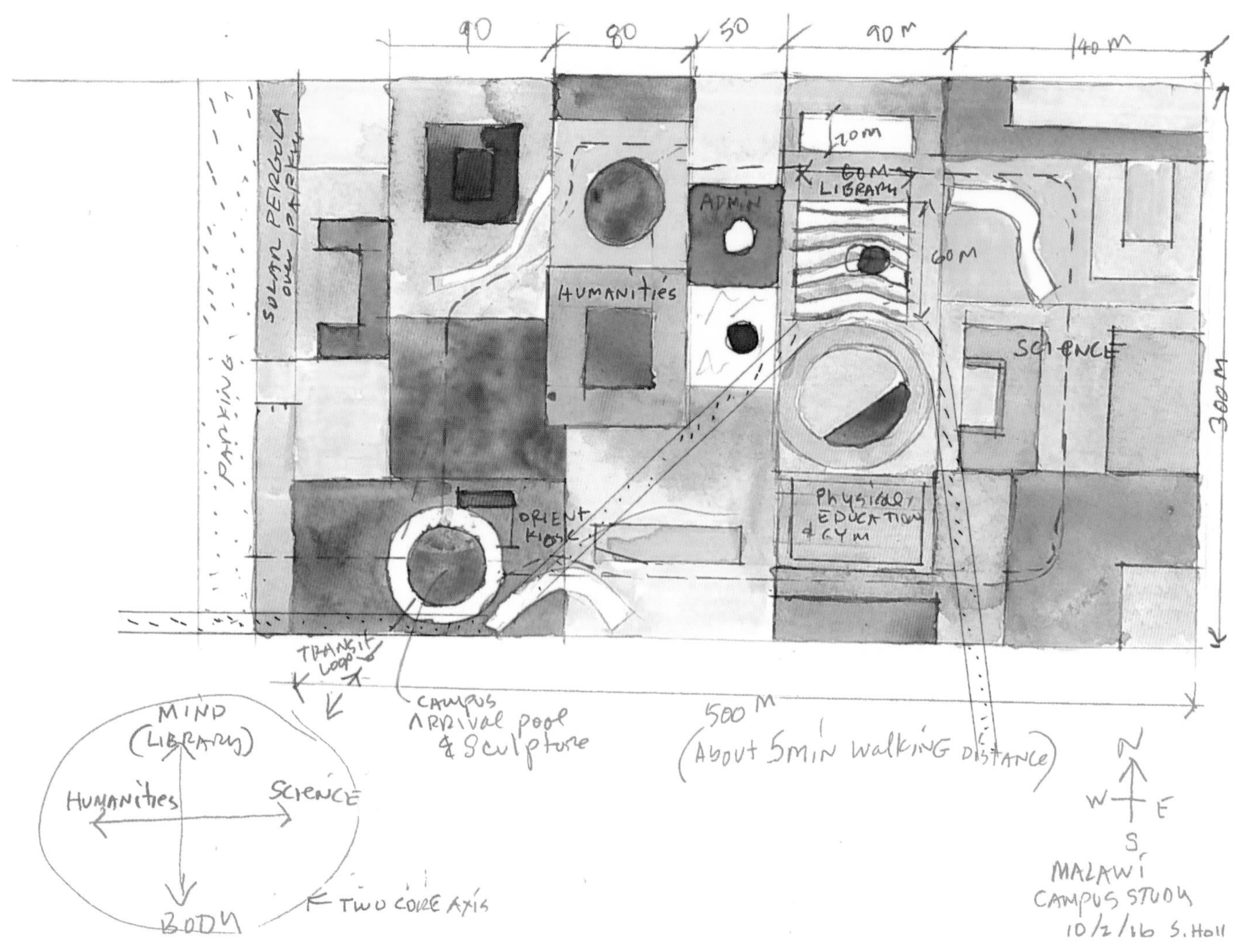

Sketch of proposed campus master plan shows a concentrated density for pedestrian use, with roughly a five-minute walk from building to building.

The geometry was based on Malawian batik artwork, to be realized in landscaping and future buildings.

MALAWI LIBRARY AND DORMITORY

Lilongwe, Malawi
2016–

Malawi, called "the warm heart of Africa," has a population of 16.7 million. Among the smallest countries in Africa, it is also one of the world's most underdeveloped, with the lowest income per person worldwide.

This project began with the goal of maximizing solar energy and natural light. Our longtime consultant Matthias Schuler of Transsolar made the first sketch concerning maximum light and solar photovoltaics.

The client, Y. K. Chung, founder and chairman of the Miracle for Africa Foundation, made the following comments following the design presentation:

> There is great excitement about this project as an artistic masterpiece and about the solar energy concept as it works with maximal light, ventilation, and humidity control. I'm astonished at the consideration and interpretation of Malawian batik art, the reflective pool, waves in a field of light, and the philosophical axes of the campus. This project is historic. The library will be an iconic marker for a great moment in the architectural history of Malawi and for all of Africa—especially Malawi, which has been away from modern civilization for so long.

The 66,000-square-foot (6,132-square-meter) library is organized via a section that provides maximum reflected light to the interior with optimum solar photovoltaic collection on the roofs. Natural light bouncing off curved roof structures forms space, acting as a field within a field. The geometry of the roof ripples like a wave in African grasses.

The free-plan library has meeting rooms and archives encased in glass for humidity control. A central rain-collecting pool marks the main circulation desk.

Screens of locally crafted bamboo define the building perimeter, leaving a shaded arcade all around.

A classroom building will be realized, with the library as the first campus space.

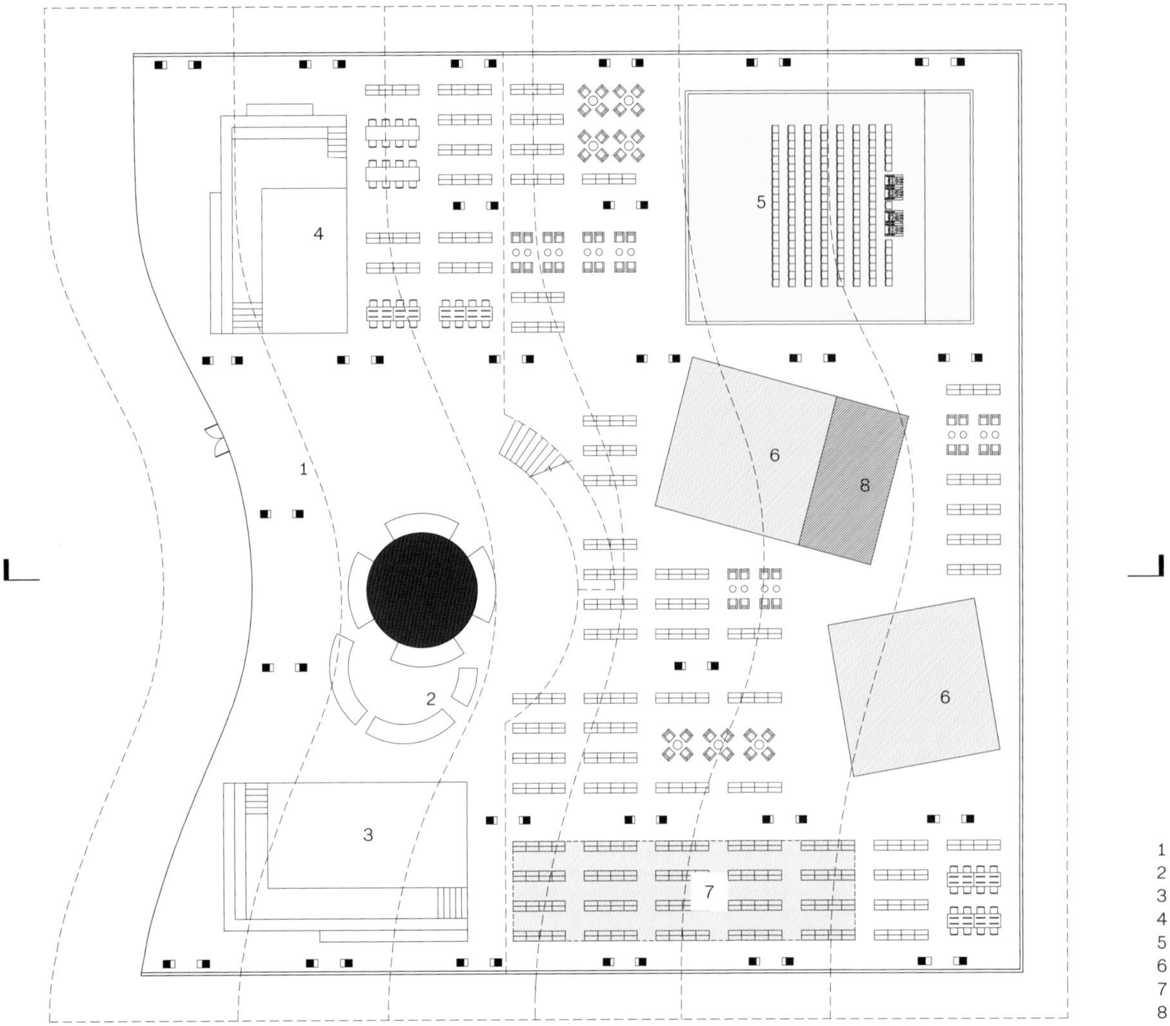

1 Lobby and Lounge
2 Information and Book Return
3 Forum (Conversation)
4 Digital Forum (Silence)
5 Conference Room
6 Seminar Room
7 Book Archive
8 Bathroom

Floor plan 20m

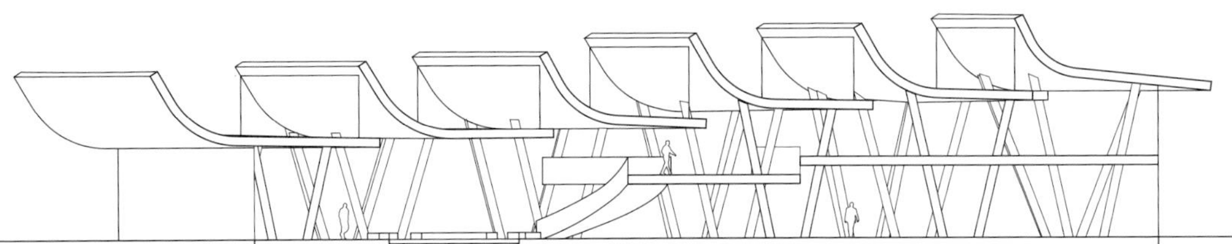

Section 20m

left
Joyous welcome dance with local citizens, showing regional uniforms and garb

above
Interior view of library

below
Library model, night view

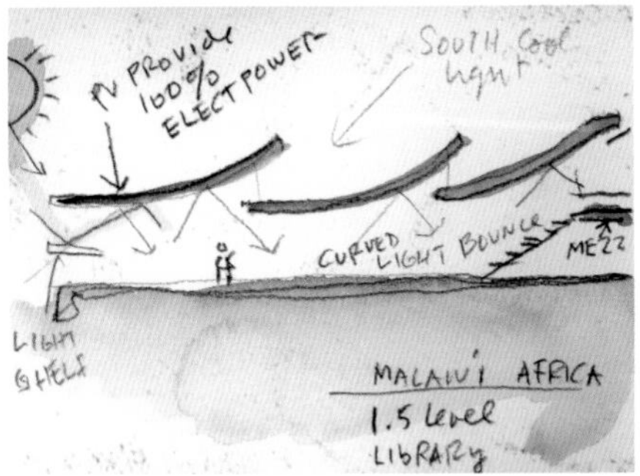

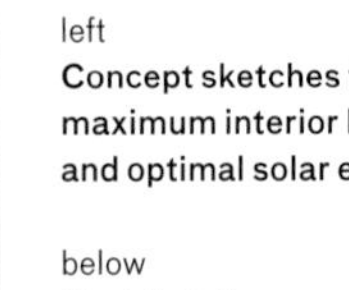

left
Concept sketches for maximum interior light and optimal solar energy

below
Model of classroom building to be realized with library

right
Plan-view model of library and classroom

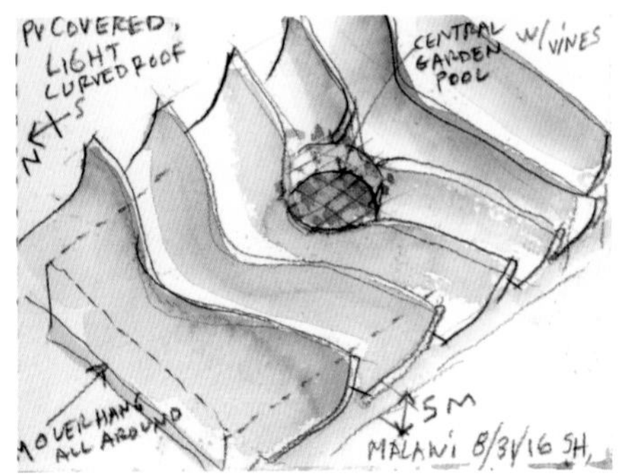

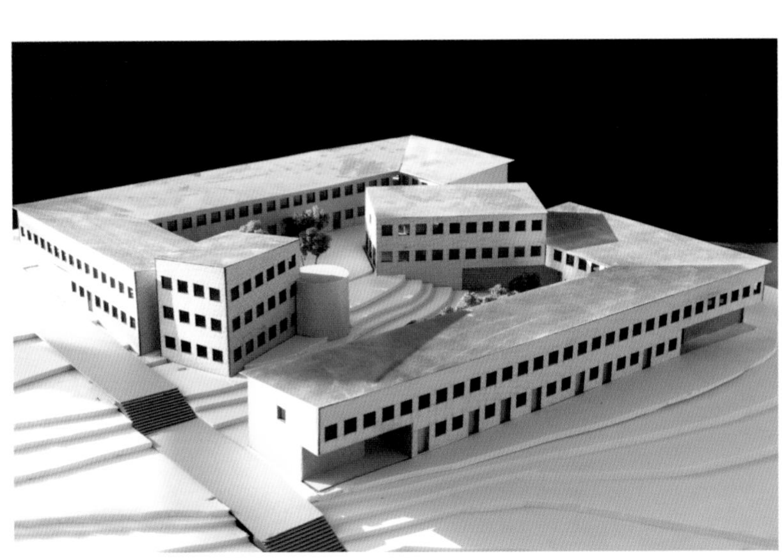

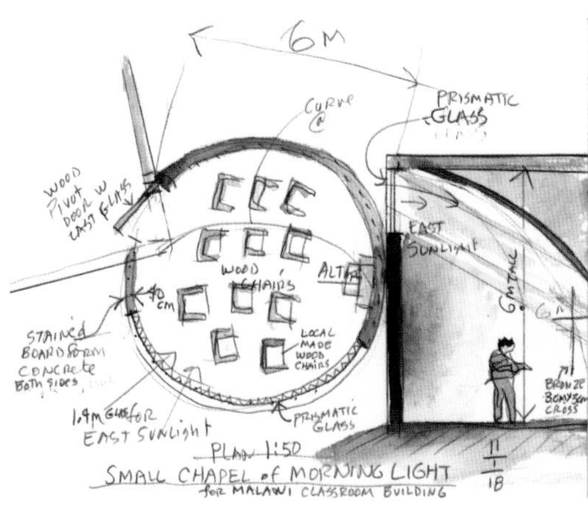

Concept watercolor
for the Chapel
of Morning Light

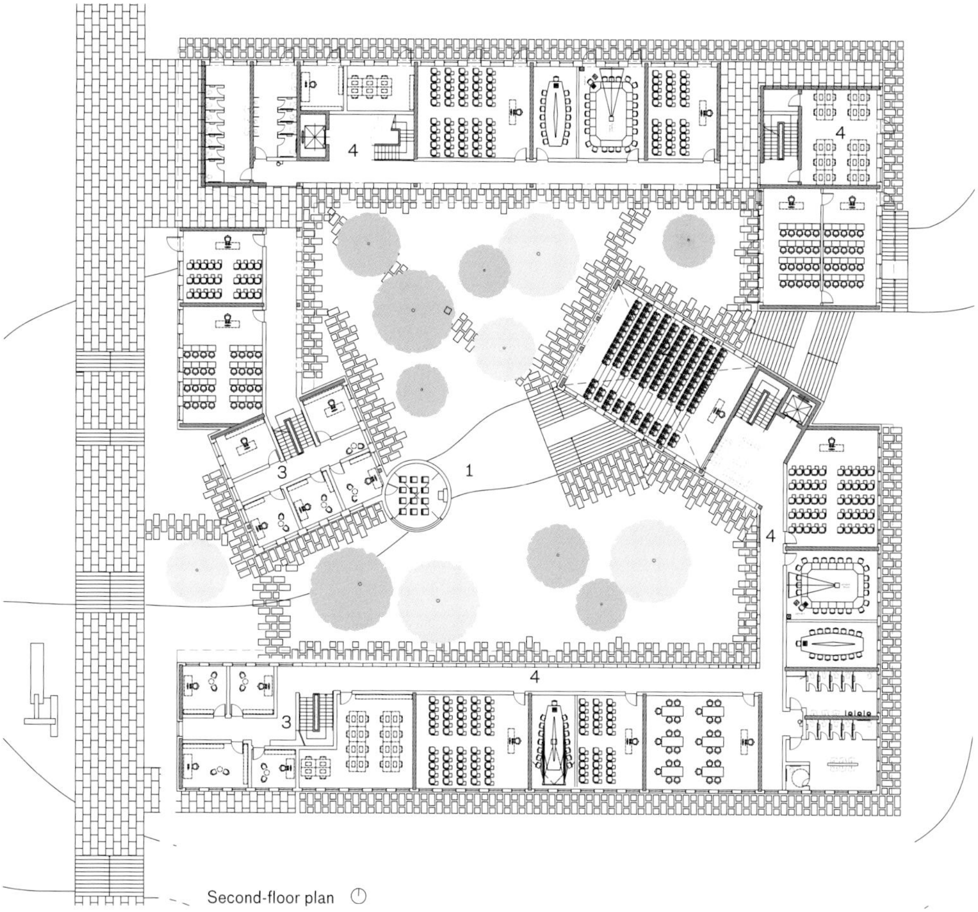

1 Chapel
2 Lecture Hall
3 Teachers' Offices
4 Classrooms

Classroom building

Second-floor plan

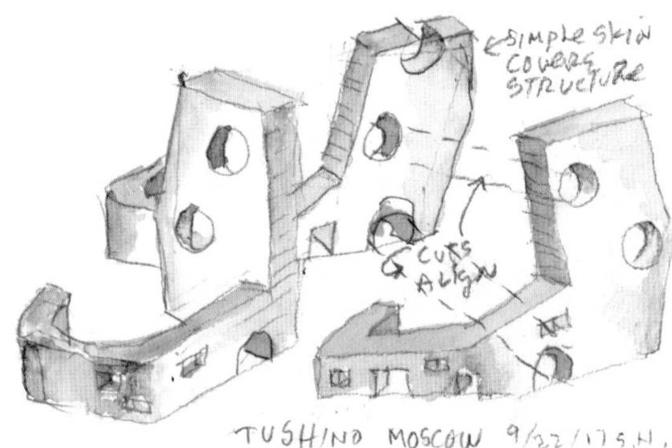

My father, Myron L. Holl, jumping as a captain in the paratroopers, 1944

PARACHUTE HYBRIDS TUSHINO DISTRICT

Moscow, Russia
2017
Competition: First Place

A new residential-tower development in the Tushino district of Moscow provides a mixed-use center filled with housing, social spaces, a kindergarten, and an elementary school on a former paratrooper airfield.

Tushino is in northwestern Moscow, along the bank of the Moscow River. For the greater part of the twentieth century, the historic site was home to a flying and parachuting school, including the Central Aero Club of the USSR, and acted as an aviation parade ground.

In the early 2000s, city officials proposed turning the uninhabited district into a two-million-square-foot (200,000-square-meter) urban center for housing, commerce, offices, entertainment, and sports. Tushino will have a mix of housing types and will provide homes for all economic brackets.

The master plan is organized to shape public space with maximum sunlight exposure. The buildings wrap around to create large public-garden and playground spaces, a reference to the site's former use as an airfield. The new kindergarten and elementary school are designed to stand alone in architecturally distinct buildings that take advantage of natural light and green space.

We proposed a new building typology that combines residential bar and slab structures with supplemental programming suspended in sections above, like parachutes frozen in the sky. Large, circular openings in the towers' facades define the project's geometric character and express health and social spaces such as health spas, pools, cafés, and lounges.

The design specifies green roofs, daylighting, rainwater recycling, and geothermal heating and cooling. Apartments will be enclosed in a thin section facade of operable glass that will help insulate the buildings in winter and create open balconies for every apartment in warmer months.

After being notified of our unanimous win on Thanksgiving Day 2017, we worked for six months with a local Moscow architect who, it seems, took over the project. From the client? Silence…

Google
Google

GARE DU NORD

Paris, France
2017
Competition

As part of the planned transformation of Paris for the 2024 Olympics, our concept for the Gare du Nord renovation and expansion is a "crystal cloud" floating over the original train station. This new departure hall is an embracing space formed of intersecting spheres that bring natural light into the station, adding new areas for commercial businesses, services, catering, and co-working centers. It frees up space below for all arrival traffic to flow directly into the main level from the platforms of the original station. The cloudlike, intersecting spheres, made of precast ductile concrete with slices of matte sandblasted glass, produce an inspiring and iconic space that complements and contrasts the original 1866 space by architect Jacques Ignace Hittorff.

For the 2024 Olympics, a temporary tower of light is formed of the five intersecting Olympic rings as intersecting spheres: an Okalux facade like stained glass is in the colors of humanity and issues a glowing invitation at night.

Our conceptual strategy of the crystal cloud (90 percent of which could be constructed in prefabricated pieces off-site) would make it unnecessary to close off the Gare du Nord, the busiest railway station in Europe.

vimeo.com/307768685

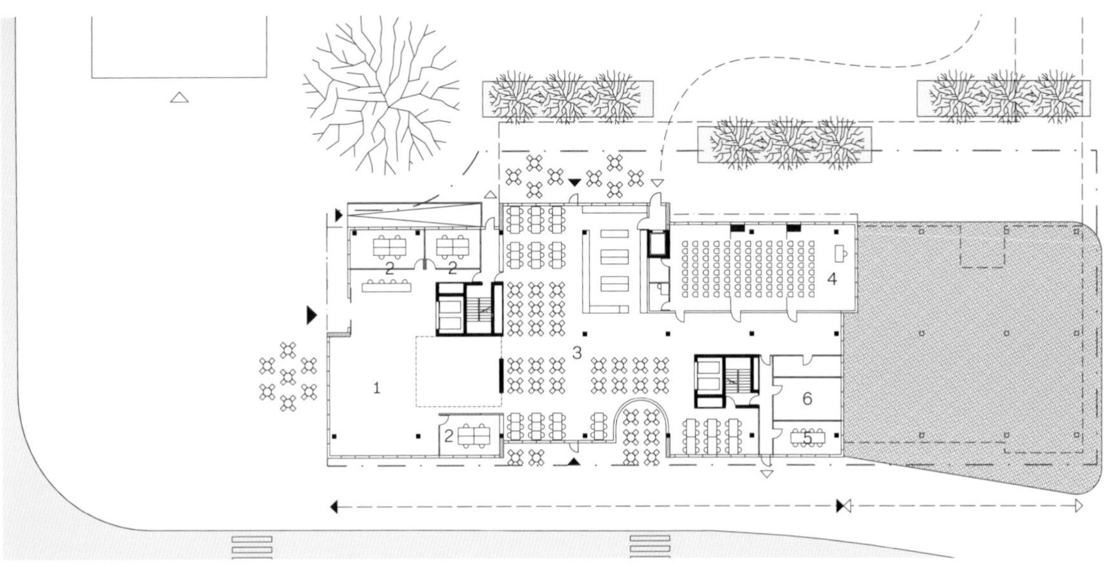

1 Exhibition
2 Office
3 Café
4 Auditorium
5 Meeting room
6 Storage

Site with future expansion to the east

MÉDECINS SANS FRONTIÈRES (DOCTORS WITHOUT BORDERS) HEADQUARTERS

Geneva, Switzerland
2017–18
Competition: First Place

Three basic concepts organize this 90,000-square-foot (8,361-square-meter) facility: "open-ended flexibility" is expressed in the cubic geometry of the building, which can be added to in the future and which hosts changing multicultural programs. "Crisscrossing circulation" encourages open interaction among Médecins Sans Frontières (Doctors Without Borders) and all who work in the building; passages are lined with casual seating alcoves and coffee places. "Colors of humanity" is expressed in the photovoltaics embedded in the fritted colors of the curtain wall. This new application of colored ceramic frit with photovoltaics, developed with Matthias Schuler, would provide 75 percent of the electricity for the building.

We won this competition by unanimous vote in December 2017.

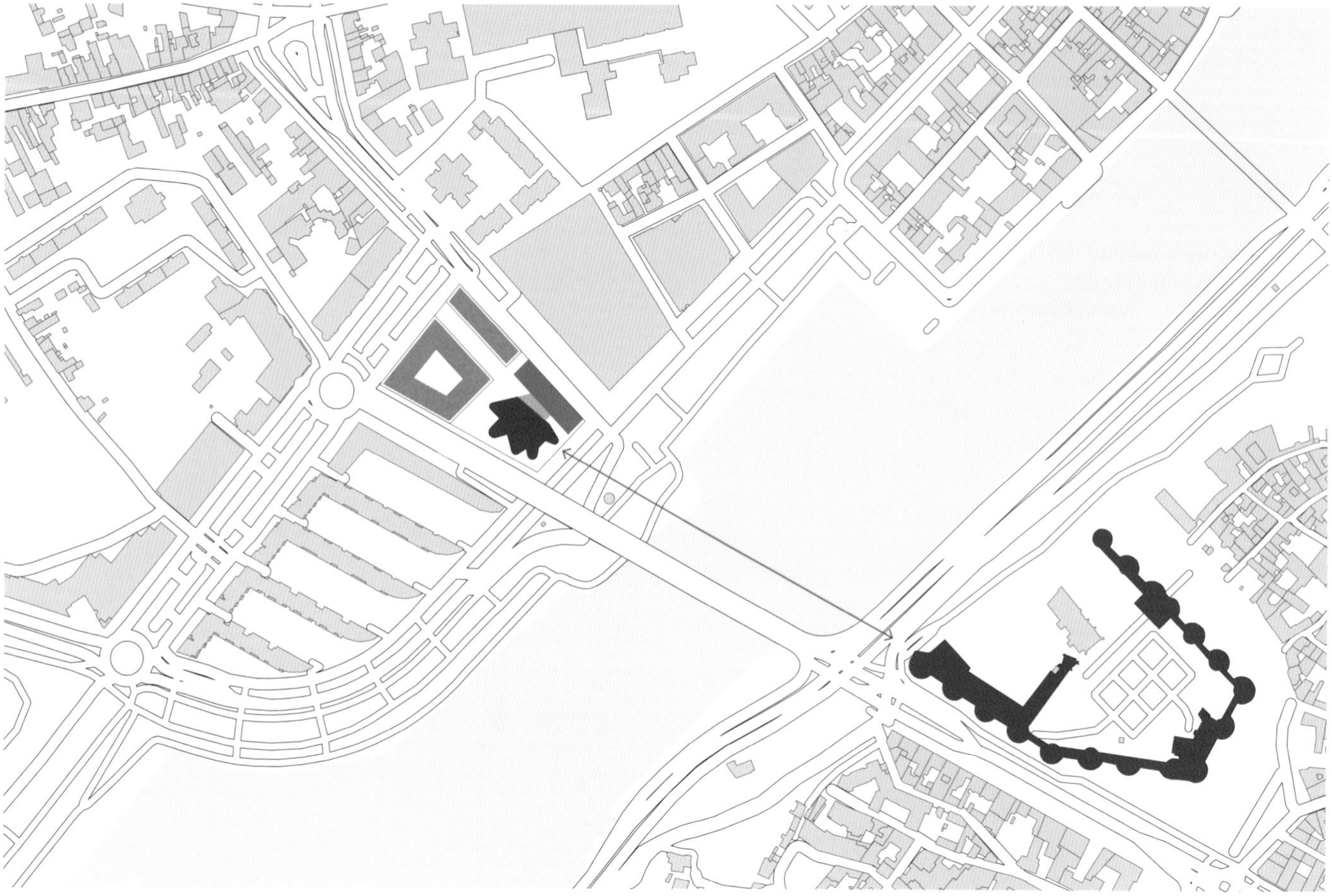

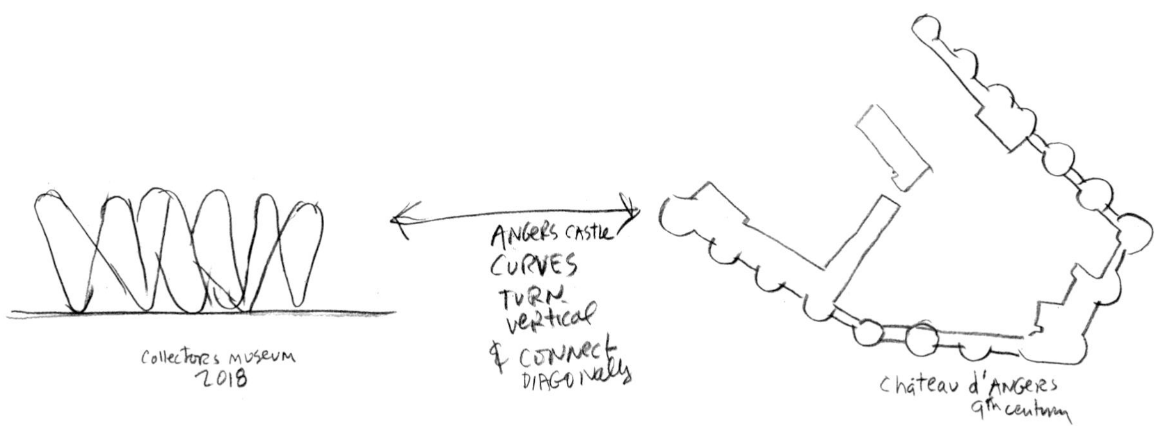
Collectors museum
2018
ANGERS CASTLE
CURVES
TURN
vertical
& CONNECT
DIAGONally
Château d'ANGERS
9th century

IMAGINE ANGERS COLLECTORS MUSEUM AND HOTEL

Angers, France

2017–21

Competition: First Place

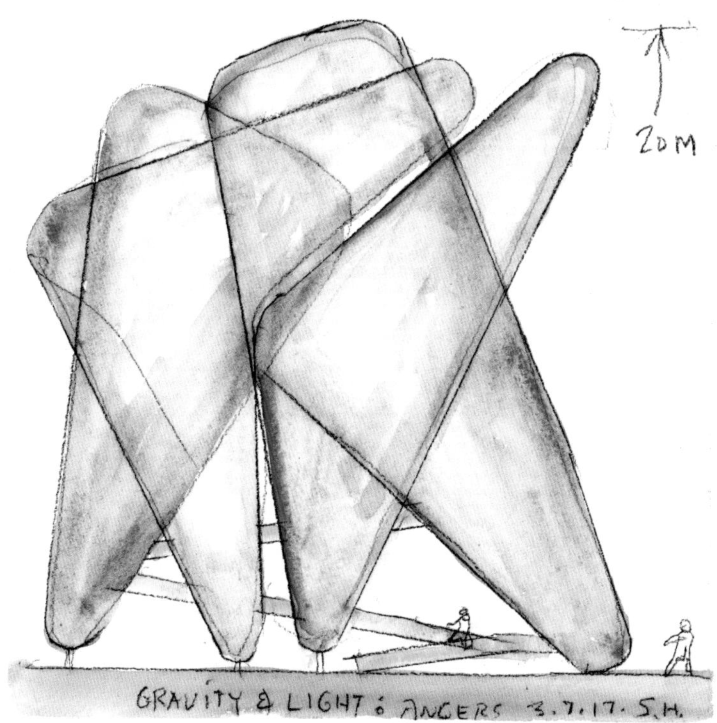

Early concept sketch

A public museum to house private art collections and an adjacent restaurant and hotel will rise on a site in the center of the city. The geometry of the new building, located across from the Château d'Angers, begins like the curved elements of the château plan's, extruding vertically into nearly orthogonal galleries.

The new adjacent hotel is like a long pixelated tapestry of translucent glass, inspired by the fourteenth-century Apocalypse Tapestry—one of the longest in the world—on display within the château.

vimeo.com/261283092

left
Study model, August 2018

below
Collector's Museum Lobby

Floor plan 10m

1 Entry
2 Lobby
3 Event Space
4 Temporary Gallery
5 Auditorium
6 Children's Education
7 Commercial
8 Restaurant
9 Gift Shop
10 Office
11 Meeting
12 Pool

Possibly more than any other element, water is the complete poetic reality.
—GASTON BACHELARD
WATER AND DREAMS, 1942

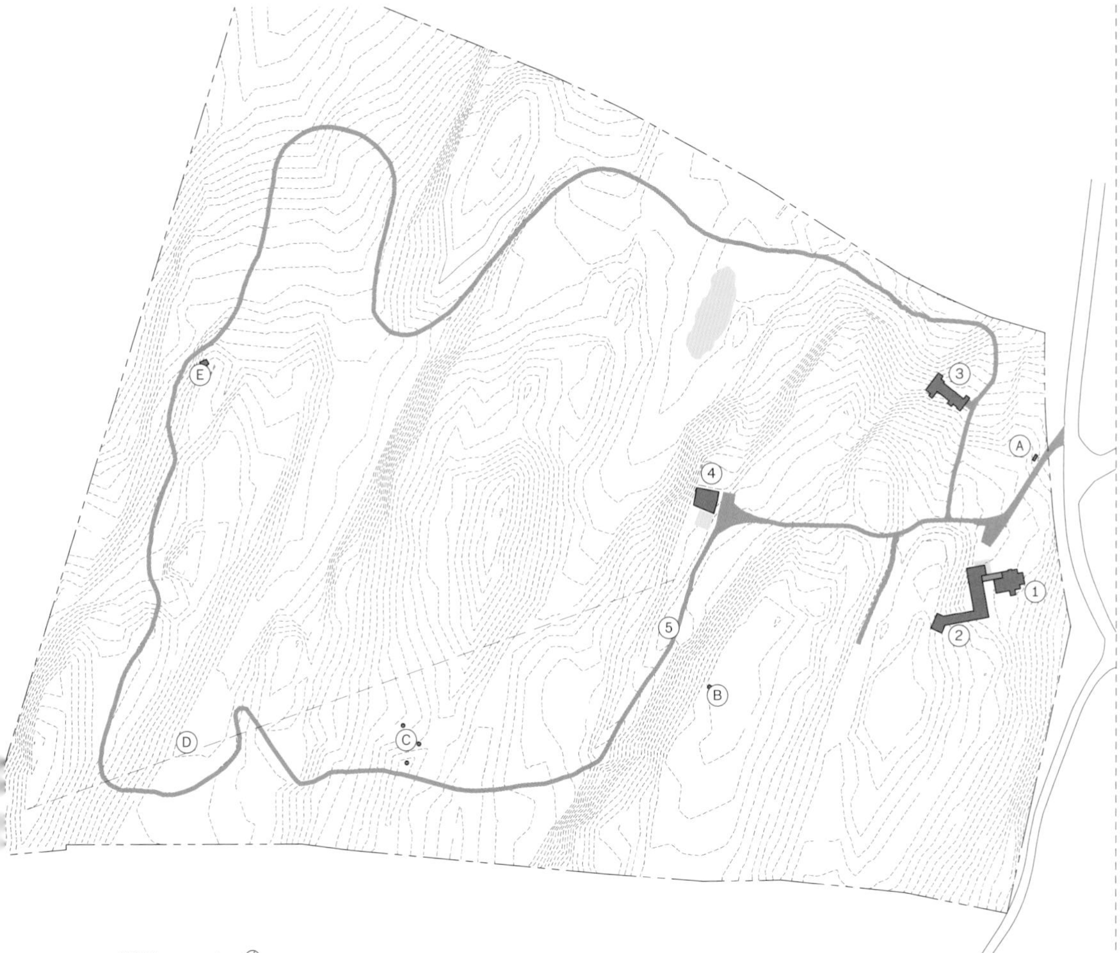

T2 Reserve plan

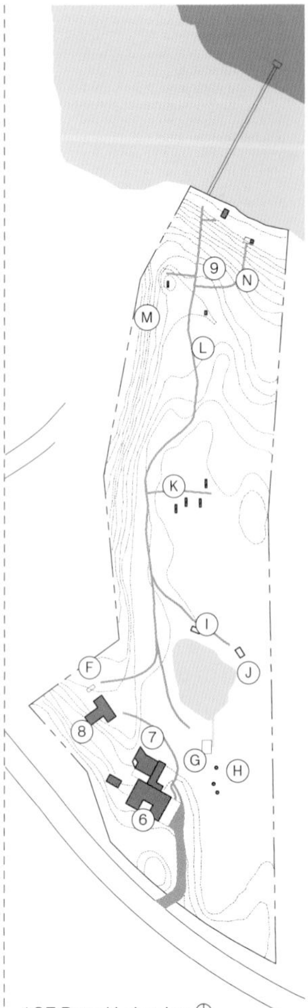

137 Round Lake plan

T2 Reserve

1 Cabin
2 Archive / Library
3 T2 Studio
4 Ex of IN House
5 T2 Sculpture Trail
A *Cold Jacket*, Steven Holl
B *Chapel of the Mosquitoes*, Jose Oubrerie
C *SUSTAIN / ABILITY*, Dimitra Tsachrelia, Eirini Tsachrelia, Nicholas Karytinos
D *WHERE NONE**, Richard Nonas
E *Tent*, Oscar Tuazon

137 Round Lake

F *Rabbit / Spoon*, Mike Metz
G Frog's Deck
H *Three Stones*, Javier Gomez
I *Bronze Watercolor*, Steven Holl
J *Cone of Water*, Meg Webster
K *8 Sounds Reversal*, *Air Space Reversal*, Steven Holl
L *Xonan*, Steven Holl
M *Wrench / Sled*, Mike Metz
N *Sitting*, Richard Artschwager
6 Stone 'U' House
7 Little Tesseract
8 'T' Space
9 Round Like Hut

Ex of IN House
vimeo.com/199345992

ARCHITECTURE ARCHIVE AND RESEARCH LIBRARY

Rhinebeck, New York
2017–19

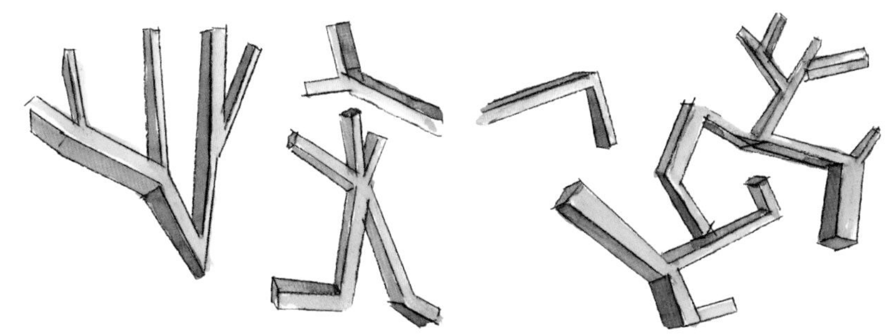

Brachiating time is expressed with the addition of a new architecture that contrasts with an existing building.

The definition of *brachiate*, "to move by using arms to swing from branch to branch," is apt for this architectural archive and research library, envisioned in branching sections. Threading through the site's existing trees, the new extension is anchored by a bungalow built around 1940.

From the entry, the Archive and Library heads south for 60 feet (18 meters), then turns west up a slope to a loading dock 10 feet (3 meters) higher than the main entrance.

The structure is heated and cooled via a single geothermal 500-foot-deep (152-meter) well and has radiant concrete floors. The superinsulated construction features a green roof and is lit entirely by natural light through seven high-tech skylights donated by the Velux Foundations. (Steven Holl was awarded the Daylight Award for Architecture by the Velux Foundations in 2017.) The 2,763-square-foot (257-square-meter) structure has a special fine-grain mill-finish aluminum skin.

The facility will hold the Steven Holl Architects archive and serve as an education and research center, adjacent to the 30-acre T2 Reserve and Sculpture Trail.

The T2 Reserve saved its 30-acre site from becoming a five-house subdivision in 2014. Also located on the reserve, the experimental Ex of IN House was realized with geothermal heating and solar electric power. This 915-square-foot (85-square-meter) house was built by Javier Gomez's team in eleven months. Nearby, a 1950s hunting shack was transformed into a studio for the Summer Architecture Residency program, which began in 2017.

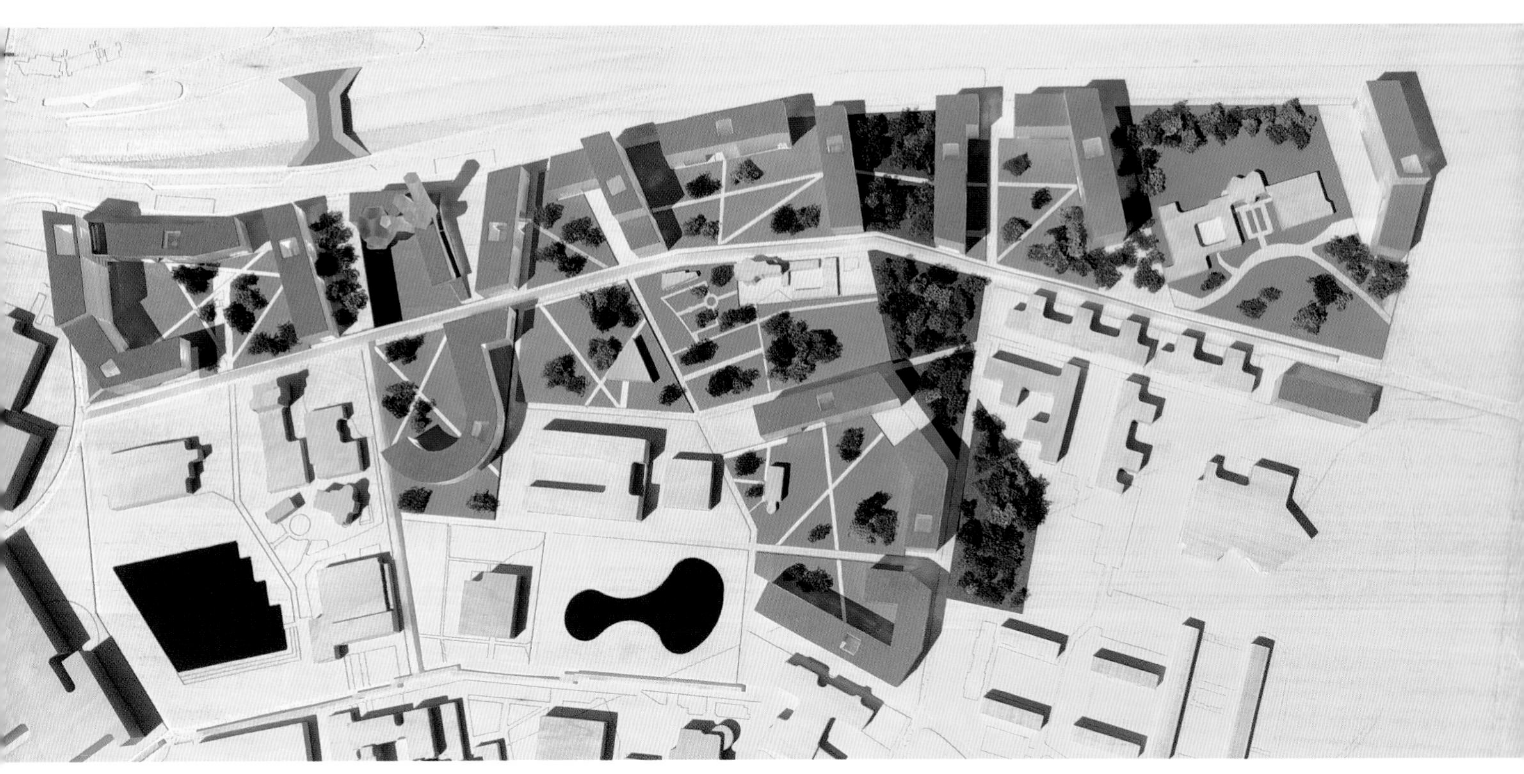

Seven quadrangles of the master plan shape campus spaces with a landscape variety. Thin sections bring light and natural ventilation to all spaces.

UNIVERSITY COLLEGE DUBLIN FUTURE CAMPUS EXPANSION

Dublin, Ireland
2018

Competition: First Place

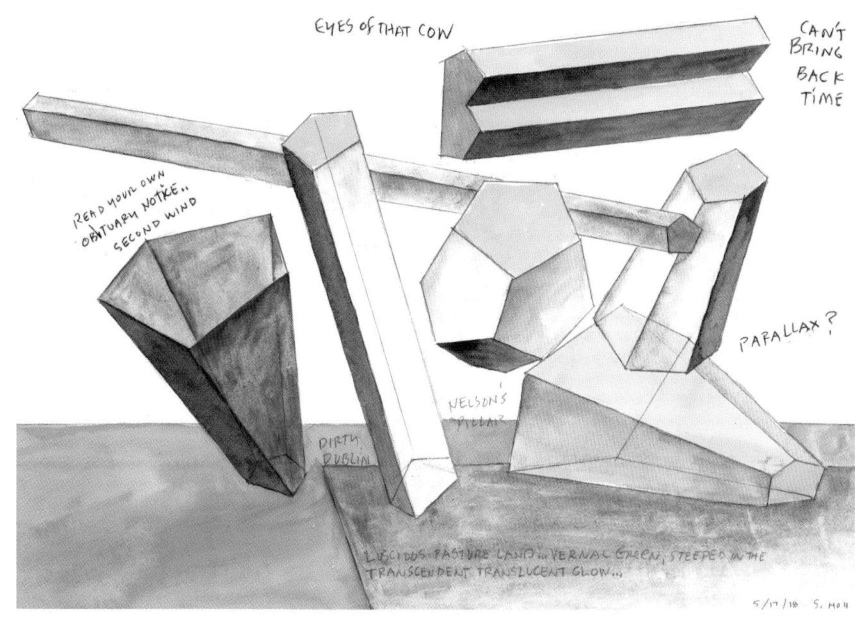

Envisioning a unique gateway building of 80,000 square feet (7,432 square meters), we found inspiration in University College Dublin alumnus James Joyce's stream-of-consciousness technique of writing, the idea of openness, and Ireland's Giant's Causeway—a sixty-million-year-old geometry of cooling lava that formed natural 120-degree hexagons.

These concepts, brought together in teleological suspension, are shaped into a horizontal organization of architecture with emerging studios, classrooms, a 450-seat auditorium, maker spaces, a cafe, a large entry forum, and an observation tower. The observation tower is tilted vertically to match the Earth's axis (23 degrees) and has an observation space overlooking the sea with a GPS telescope for cosmic explorations.

The master plan comprises seven quadrangles formed in relation to existing historic buildings. This important historical connection celebrates the unique site.

Our "H Plan" extends the original covered walkways as an "H Section." It is also the infrastructure for our nearly-net-zero concept for providing the energy for the campus. Pedestrian campus porosity is integral to the design. Every hundred feet (thirty meters) can be moved through in all different directions on footpaths that connect buildings. Pedestrian routes in the building are open to the studios, creating a circuit of social connection.

Presentation video: vimeo.com/288808214

Ireland is known as the Emerald Isle. Because of its clouds and rain, a glowing building makes for glowing streets.

right
The Giant's Causeway's sixty-million-year-old natural geometry

far right
The observation tower at the tilt of the Earth's axis, 23 degrees

below
Cast-zinc model of the Center for Creative Design, a gateway building to the new campus

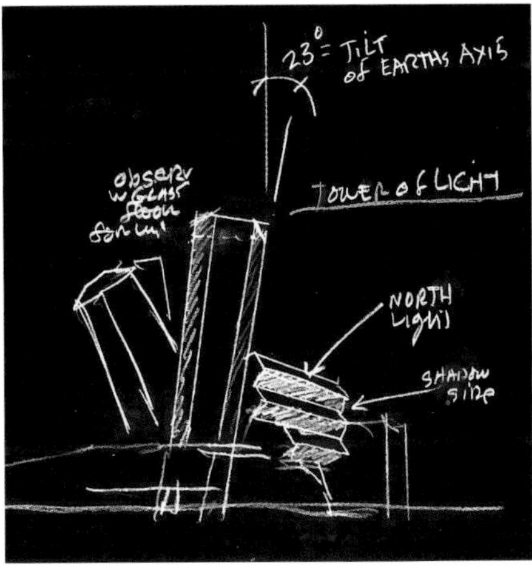

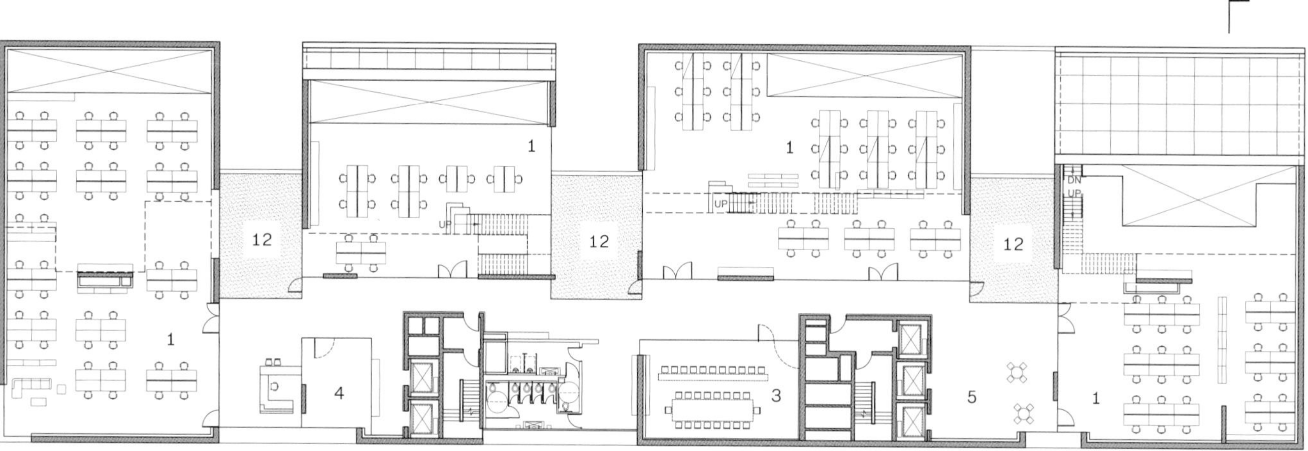

Sixth-floor plan

CIFI OFFICE BUILDING

Beijing, China
2018–

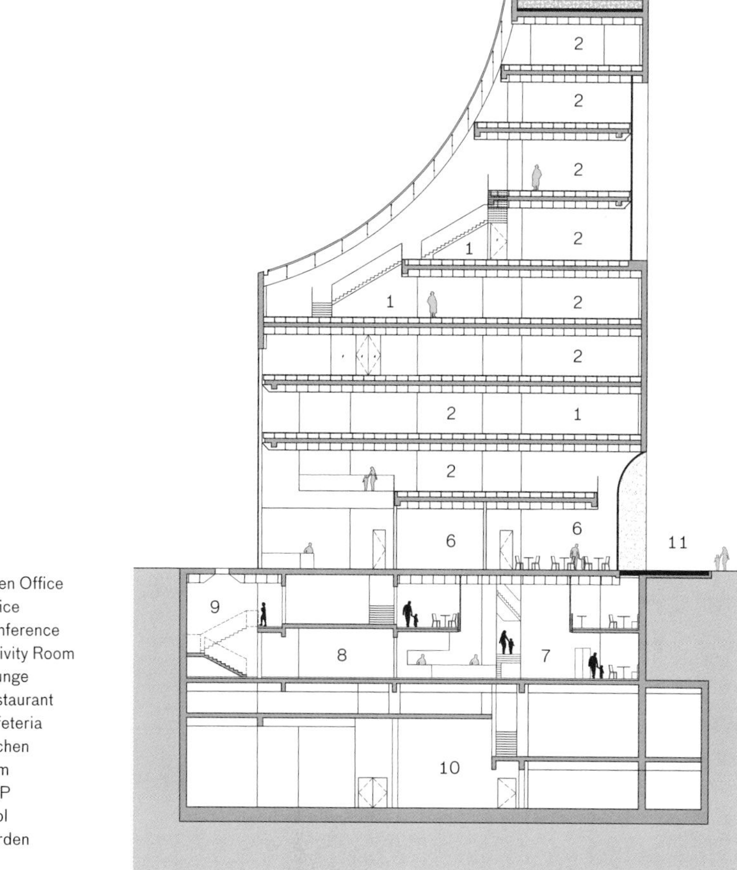

1 Open Office
2 Office
3 Conference
4 Activity Room
5 Lounge
6 Restaurant
7 Cafeteria
8 Kitchen
9 Gym
10 MEP
11 Pool
12 Garden

Qualities of light give this office and retail building a unique geometry and inspiring spaces. The north light curves—in response to code setback requirements—provide soft, even, and diffused light to the flexible interiors.

On the south facade, sculpted cuts bring south light to the office spaces and to retail below grade.

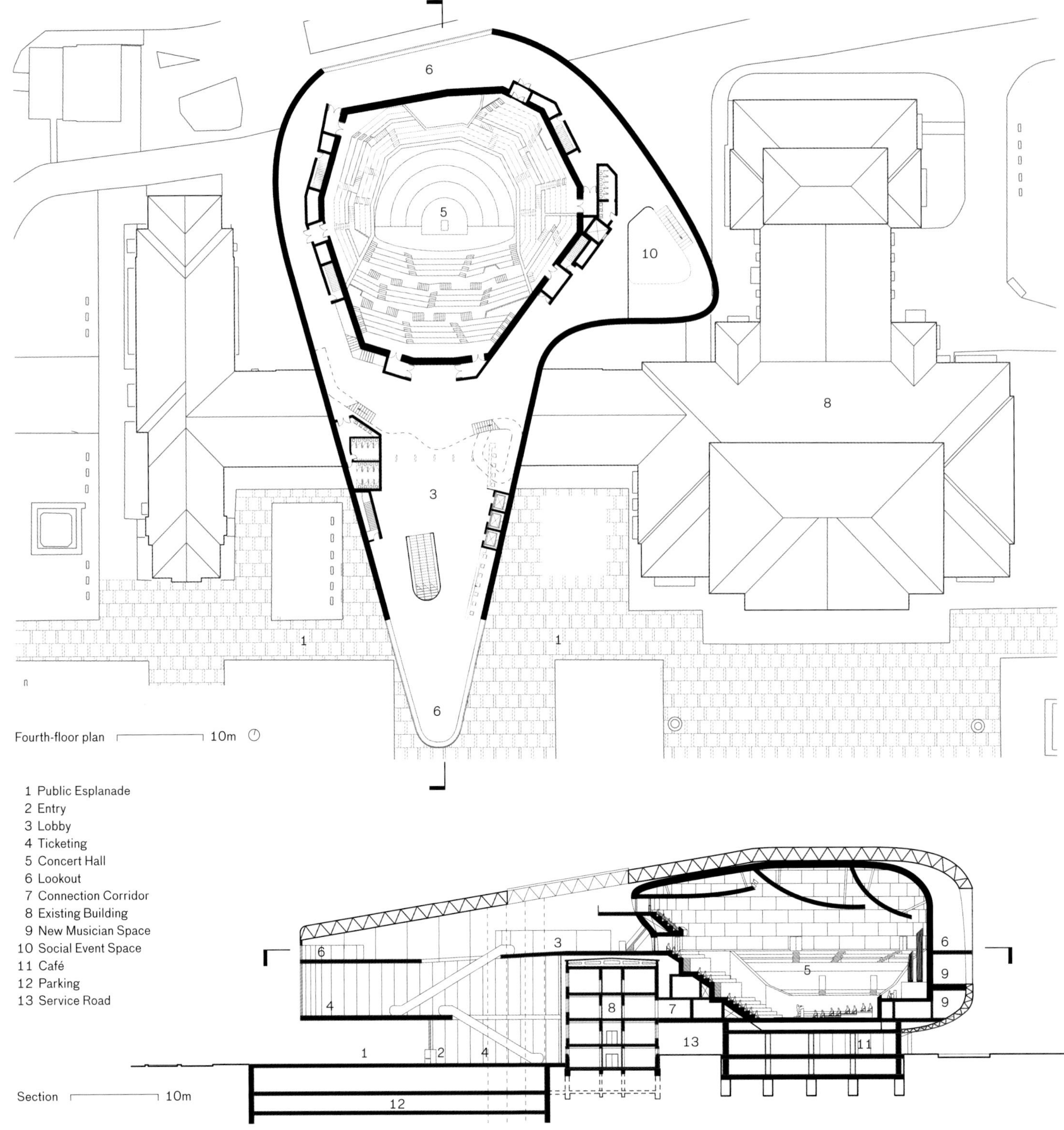

Fourth-floor plan

Section

1 Public Esplanade
2 Entry
3 Lobby
4 Ticketing
5 Concert Hall
6 Lookout
7 Connection Corridor
8 Existing Building
9 New Musician Space
10 Social Event Space
11 Café
12 Parking
13 Service Road

OSTRAVA CONCERT HALL

Ostrava, Czech Republic
2018–
Competition: First Place

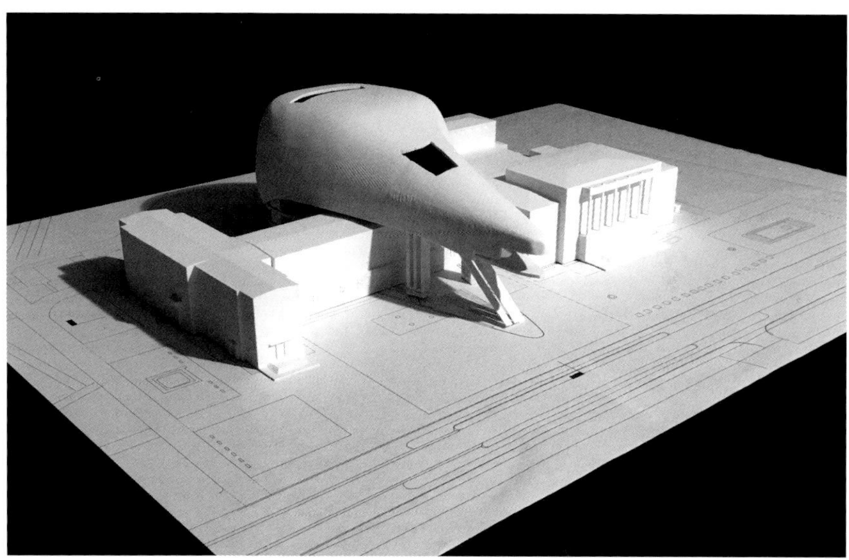

Janáček Philharmonic Orchestra is the leading Czech orchestra for commissioning contemporary music. The city of Ostrava is planning to build a new thirteen-hundred-seat concert hall adjacent to an existing nineteenth-century cultural center. We proposed the concept of a perfect acoustic instrument in its case, with the guidance of Nagata Acoustics, Paris.

The smooth, iconic steel case holds its "instrument" in an extended vineyard-type plan made of concrete and maple wood. Czech composer Leoš Janáček's theories of time guide and give order to the concert hall's interior geometry. Acoustic wall panels are organized according to *časování*, or rhythm, in three variants:

1. *znici* = sounding
2. *citaci* = counting
3. *scelovac* = summing

The Concert Hall faces the existing park to the north, thus minimizing noise from the main boulevard to the south. A new entrance hovers over the esplanade and transports the public above the historic House of Culture into a skylit lobby for the concert hall.

The concert hall in the "city of steel" is constructed in prefabricated steel truss-work to allow for minimum disruption of the existing building operation. Off-site fabrication will reduce construction time on site by half.

The dramatic complementary contrast of old and new creates a cultural landmark for Ostrava. The new architecture points to the future of the city.

1.

2.

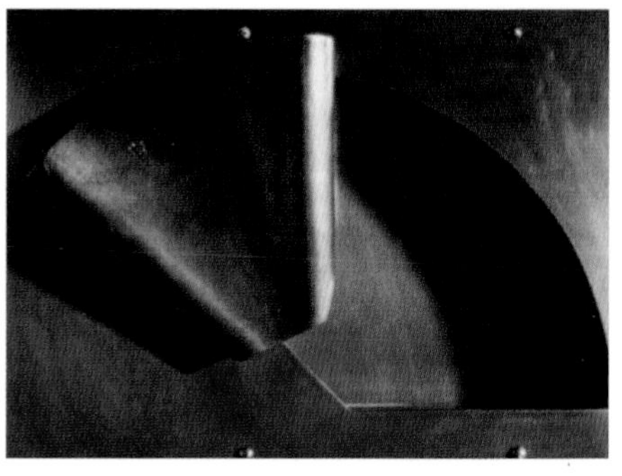

3.

Writing is literally an existential process; it uses thinking for its own ends.
—JOSEPH BRODSKY
LESS THAN ONE, 1986

NON-CONCLUSION

My 2009 book, *Urbanisms: Working with Doubt*, focused on the macro and concerns of the environment. In this book, the focus is on the micro: architecture activating the brain and the importance of expressions of inner vision.

On the macro scale, our Edge of the City projects argued that preservation and restoration of the natural landscape are as urgent as new inventions of inspired urban densities. Compression of human habitat should be a concern of all global citizens living on this fragile planet. In my junior year at the University of Washington, in 1970, together with four colleagues, I started the Environmental Works. The world's population at that time was exactly half of today's 7.6 billion. In 2030 it will expand to 8.6 billion; in 2050, 9.7 billion. (One cause for optimism is that the population growth rate in 2018 was 1.09% —nearly half the rate of the 1960s.)

Architecture, planning, and environmental preservation play a decisive role in a positive future. They are antientropic inventions of humanity.

The micro scale, the neglected human scale of today, can be reached via the arts and culture of our time.

The urban library, for example, is vital as a community building, a social condenser. The pragmatist's argument that the digital is eliminating the analog misses the key forces that a free, open, public building can provide as a space where people can interact across generations.

Likewise, the art museum has become one of the most powerful urban buildings of our time—a true social condenser of art and cultural education in an open, democratic society.

We collaborated with choreographer Jessica Lang on the performance *Tesseracts of Time*, which premiered November 5, 2015, at the Harris Theater in Chicago and has now been performed in more than fifteen theaters globally. Compression of time is central to this work, as space and time are key elements of both architecture and dance. Architecture is an art of long duration; dance temporally short.

The haptic realm is at the essence of the experience of architecture. When the materiality of the details forming an architectural space become evident, the haptic realm is opened. Sensory experience is intensified; psychological dimensions are engaged.

4.

5.

6.

Compression was the main focus of the 1987 Giada showroom we made on Madison Avenue (now destroyed). The project was situated under a large building that bore down with more than gravitational force. Economic pressure and the pressure of time together act like a vise grip, pressing the space in a psychological densification. Our idea was to express compression on the exterior and relieve it in the interior through experimental details.

The infinitely small led to reflections on the infinitely large in our 2018 'T' Space summer fellowship project, *Rural Compression: Cosmic Dust*. Five international students were assigned a one-month studio problem focused on designing a small residence / observatory for an astrophysicist writing a book disputing the big bang theory of the universe's origin. We studied cosmic inflation, which explains why the universe appears to be the same in all directions (isotropic), and studied new scientific evidence of black holes at the center of galaxies.

When discussing the accelerating expansion of the universe, scientific reports describe the scientists of the inflationary model as architects. Some new models propose that the exponential expansion of the universe was, is, "and always will be spatially infinite and has existed and will exist forever," as described by John Hussey in *Bang to Eternity and Betwixt: Cosmos.*

A 2017 scientific report that humans are undeniably composed of cosmic dust (based on data from the Sloan Digital Sky Survey conducted at Apache Point Observatory in New Mexico) connects the infinitely large with the infinitely small; the macro and micro float together, blown by the wind, expanding, contracting, hovering, with no beginning and no end.

Steven Holl
Rhinebeck, New York
September 2018

1.
Jessica Lang Dance performing *Tesseracts of Time*, created by Jessica Lang and Steven Holl, at the world premiere performance at the Harris Theater for Music and Dance on November 5, 2015

2.
Giada showroom, interior

3.
Giada showroom, door pull

4.
Light-fixture test: space curve intersections in blown glass by Michael Haddy

5. and 6.
***Rural Compression: Cosmic Dust*, 2017, 2018**

THE ANALOGICAL RELATION

Sanford Kwinter

The signature principle of Steven Holl's work is the revealing to direct perception of the vivid yet undisclosed materiality of the void.[1] The void is endlessly presented as not only a constitutive firmness, by turns obdurate, viscous, plastic, tractable, saturated, or diffuse, but as an always active one: moving, mixing, brachiating—in sum, as an endless living modulation and production of relations.

We mustn't take for granted, however, how this transfer takes place. Holl's unfolding engagement with the relations between architecture and brain marks, among other things, the larger historical turn by those earnestly interested in the phenomenological problem of the structure of experience toward the new neurobiological models of how the senses, on one side, and the sensible world, on the other, functionally and inventively interlace.

To understand *Compression* we must first remind ourselves what was activated in Holl's earlier formulation *Anchoring*.[2] The anchor was developed as a device to permit something virtual found in a context or surround to be actualized in a building, to serve at once as a "copula" and as a "generative seed," a twin operation of conjoining and unfolding. By means of an anchor, a route is established for an impetus discovered natively in a site—discoverable in every site—to be developmentally transferred into a building project. As much as this is an affirmation of a real metabolism operating in the art of design, it is also a repudiation of traditional abstract models that divide matter from the processes of direct sensation (rationalism, historicism, deconstruction, et cetera). Holl's early phenomenology may well have been the first fully antitranscendent project in American postwar architecture.

Anchoring is transmitting. It is also a form of extraction or reading and hence of expression.[3] What we find, in fact, is a relation grasped, transferred, and redeployed. It is not the site itself or any practical part thereof that is put in play but rather a dynamism or potential latent within it that is isolated for animation within an artificial medium or frame. The building originates itself out of the site in what is tantamount to an embryology: a process of individuating what is not yet individual.

L'individuation du réel extérieur au sujet est saisie par le sujet grâce à l'individuation analogique de la connaissance dans le sujet.
—GILBERT SIMONDON, *L'INDIVIDU ET SA GENÈSE PHYSICO-BIOLOGIQUE*

In the above quote, from the midcentury French philosopher Gilbert Simondon, the entities through which the world presents itself are affirmed twice, not as objects, nouns, or things but as processes of articulation, expression, and refinement. To render this reading simply in English:

"The [individuation of] *reality* outside the subject is graspable only by an analogical process of individuation of the *knowledge* within the subject itself." (italics mine)

In this short but loaded half-sentence several assertions are made. The overall structure of the statement is to declare something about how our sensations of knowing/feeling/experiencing are connected to the things known/felt/experienced. The first are generally understood to be occurrences happening within us, while the second are provocatively presented as occurrences or events actively happening outside us. The apprehension or capture of the one system by the other is characterized as taking place through an analogical relation. But the symmetry of relations that the sentence organizes tells us yet something more: that the two processes carry the identical term—*individuation*—and hence the knowing/feeling/experiencing is a parallel, and ultimately even reciprocal, act of sympathetic or harmonic engagement.

Is this a musical relation? Perhaps—like the involuntary capture of a tune overheard in the street and its continual replaying in the mind throughout the day. And, likewise, it is difficult to situate the musical fact or object in the first place—is music in the world where the resonance originates or in the bodymind that traps it, recognizes it, and organizes it in dance, in expressed pattern, and in agitated memory? We know that a sound's neurological signal can be isolated from the brain and amplified, only to discover that the stimulus transiting through the gray matter bears the same untransformed structure as it does when disturbing molecules in the air around us. (This is not the case with other modalities of sensation such as touch or vision, nor do the latter activate our bodies and emotions in quite the same way.)

Holl describes what he calls the method of analogical thinking using a closely allied set of terms: *fusing*, *reciprocity*, *correlation*, *symbiosis*, *interlocking*, and *mortised equivalence*—all terms expressing conjunction or interpenetration and continuity of interior experience and exterior space, of which the latter can be that of building, landscape, or urban manifold.[4] But the analogical relation is more than this still—it represents an effective "conceptual promiscuity" of relations, or rather the transposability of relations from one setting or milieu to another, without positing a homogeneity of substance—the material is not analogous, rather the structuring processes are—or limit of application.

Architecture both receives and transmits; it places itself in active relation to sculpture, to painting, to music, and indeed even to philosophy and science.[5] To design, Holl says, is "to link," but with the provision that all linking is physical transmission and maturation of both the signal and the matter at once. One architecture can link and transmit another, but the focus in the present work is not only the transmission of form and structure from site to project, or from one art, practice, or discipline to another, but from world to bodymind...and back again.

Humans, and humans alone, shape and reshape the environments that shape their brains.
—BRUCE WEXLER
BRAIN AND CULTURE

Wexler's assertion above is based on the implications of the foundational new understanding of the environmental sculpting of our brains, as described in the theories of neural plasticity and the secondary repertoire. These doctrines argue that, in a phenomenon unique to the human brain, an extensive proportion of the brain is developed in response to stimulus received from the postnatal physical world and not from assumed autonomous processes within the tissues and genes themselves. The human brain is singularly and vitally dependent on real-world stimulus for its development and for the full execution of its general functions. But once the brain has developed—differentiated and individualized—by approximately its twenty-third year, it will seek a kind of metabolic accommodation with the outer world and will begin to modify and transform the world itself in order to match its sought-for internal state to conditions it can fashion or perform outside it. (Wexler uses the term *homology* to express this relation.[6]) This is, in a nutshell, the adventure of our senses as they transit through the shaped and organized exterior environment for the remainder of each and every human life. Not only the physical brain, of course, but also the mind, or rather the embodied sensory matrix, serves
as an anchor through which we connect to the world as well as to one another, be it through loves, politics, or culture.

This set of design processes represents our claim to the highest levels of human attainment—in a way, there are no others. This, then, I propose, is the ultimate meaning of compression—the full acknowledgment that the sculpting of physical reality—architecture—belongs to our urgent and perennial biological destiny.

1 Sanford Kwinter, "Plenum," in *Steven Holl: Color Light Time*, by Steven Holl (Zurich: Lars Müller Publishers, 2011), 65–89.
2 Steven Holl, *Anchoring* (New York: Princeton Architectural Press, 1991).
3 Used in the sense it was deployed by Gilles Deleuze in reference to Baruch Spinoza's metaphysics of bodies. Cf. Gilles Deleuze, *Expressionism in Philosophy: Spinoza* (New York: Zone Books, 1990).
4 See page 15.
5 Dima Stouhi, "Art Will Save Architecture, According to Steven Holl," *ArchDaily*, December 29, 2018, accessed January 15, 2019, https://www.archdaily.com/908160/, ISSN 0719-8884.
6 Bruce Wexler, "Shaping the Environments that Shape Our Brains: A Long-Term Perspective," in *Cognitive Architecture. From Bio-politics to Noo-politics. Architecture & Mind in the Age of Communication and Information*, ed. Deborah Hauptmann and Warren Neidich (Rotterdam: ZeroTen Publishers, 2010).

Hunters Point
Community Library
construction interior

STEVEN HOLL ARCHITECTS PROJECT CREDITS

HERNING MUSEUM OF CONTEMPORARY ART

Steven Holl (design architect, principal), Noah Yaffe (project architect), Chris McVoy (project adviser), Lesley Chang, Martin Cox, JongSeo Lee, Alessandro Orsini, Julia Radcliffe, Filipe Taboada, Christina Yessios (project team), Alessandro Orsini, Cosimo Caggiula (competition team)

CITÉ DE L'OCÉAN ET DU SURF

Steven Holl (design architect in collaboration with Solange Fabião), Rodolfo Dias (project architect), Filipe Taboada (assistant project architect), Chris McVoy (project adviser), Francesco Bartolozzi, Christopher Brokaw, Cosimo Caggiula, Rychiee Espinosa, Florence Guiraud, Richard Liu, Maki Matsubayashi, Johanna Muszbek, Ernest Ng, Alessandro Orsini, Nelson Wilmotte, Ebbie Wisecarver, Lan Wu, Christina Yessios (project team)

LEWIS ARTS COMPLEX PRINCETON UNIVERSITY

Steven Holl (design architect, principal), Noah Yaffe (partner in charge), Christina Yessios (project architect, associate), Nathan Rich (project architect), JongSeo Lee (senior associate), Whitney Forward (assistant project architect), Chris McVoy (project adviser), Laetitia Buchter, Bell Cai, Zach Cohen, Scott Fredricks, Michael Haddy, Jing Han, Gary He, Martin Kropac, David Alan Ross, Alfonso Simelio, Asami Takahashi, Arseni Timofejev, Yasmin Vobis, Ebbie Wisecarver (project team)

CAMPBELL SPORTS CENTER COLUMBIA UNIVERSITY

Steven Holl (design architect, principal), Chris McVoy (partner in charge), Olaf Schmidt (associate in charge), Marcus Carter, Xi Chen, Christiane Deptolla, Peter Englaender, Runar Halldorsson, Jackie Luk, Filipe Taboada, Dimitra Tsachrelia, Ebbie Wisecarver (project team)

LM HARBOUR GATEWAY

Steven Holl (design architect, principal), Noah Yaffe (partner in charge), Chris McVoy (project adviser, senior partner), Marcus Carter (associate in charge), Justin Allen, Lourenzo Amaro de Oliveira, Esin Erez, Runar Halldorsson, Suk Lee, Yu-Ju Lin, Fiorenza Matteoni, Christopher Rotman, Wenying Sun, Yan Zhang (project team), Rashid Satti (competition project architect)

DAEYANG GALLERY AND HOUSE

Steven Holl (design architect, principal), JongSeo Lee (associate in charge), Annette Goderbauer, Chris McVoy (project advisers), Francesco Bartolozzi, Marcus Carter, Nick Gelpi, Jackie Luk, Fiorenza Matteoni, Rashid Satti, Dimitra Tsachrelia (project team)

REID BUILDING GLASGOW SCHOOL OF ART

Steven Holl (design architect, principal), Chris McVoy (senior partner in charge), Noah Yaffe (partner in charge), Dominik Sigg (project architect), Dimitra Tsachrelia (assistant project architect), Rychiee Espinosa, Scott Fredricks, JongSeo Lee, Jackie Luk, Fiorenza Matteoni, Ebbie Wisecarver (project team), Peter Adams, Rychiee Espinosa, Dominik Sigg (competition team)

SHAN-SHUI HANGZHOU

Steven Holl (design architect, principal), Chris McVoy (senior partner in charge), Roberto Bannura (project director), Lan Wu (associate in charge), Michael Rusch, Garrick Ambrose (project architects), Francesco Bartolozzi, Zach Cohen, Nathalie Frankowski, Gary He, Max Kolbowski-Frampton, Pei Shyun Lee, Johanna Muszbek, Daijiro Nakayama, Jose Quelhas, Garrett Ricciardi, Wenying Sun, Human Tieliu Wu (project team), Li Hu, Garrick Ambrose, Human Tieliu Wu, Lan Wu (competition project architects), Francesco Bartolozzi, Guanlan Cao, Rychiee Espinosa, Nathalie Frankowski, Kelvin Jia, Fiorenza Matteoni, Lautaro Pereyra, Filipe Taboada, Asami Takahashi, Dimitra Tsachrelia, Ebbie Wisecarver (competition team)

HANGZHOU MUSIC MUSEUM

Steven Holl (design architect, principal), Li Hu, Chris McVoy (partners in charge), Hideki Hirahara, Guanlan Cao, Filipe Taboada, Human Tieliu Wu (project architects), Yimei Chan, Nathalie Frankowski, Kelvin Jia, Max Kolbowski-Frampton, Fiorenza Matteoni (project team)

VISUAL ARTS BUILDING UNIVERSITY OF IOWA

Steven Holl (design architect, principal), Chris McVoy (design architect, partner in charge), Rychiee Espinosa (project architect, associate), Garrick Ambrose, Bell Cai, Christine Deptolla, JongSeo Lee, Johanna Muszbek, Garrett Ricciardi, Christopher Rotman, Filipe Taboada, Christina Yessios, Yiqing Zhao, (project team)

HUNTERS POINT COMMUNITY LIBRARY

Steven Holl (design architect, principal), Chris McVoy (senior partner in charge), Olaf Schmidt (senior associate in charge), Filipe Taboada (project architect, associate), Suk Lee (assistant project architect), Bell Cai, Rychiee Espinosa, JongSeo Lee, Maki Matsubayashi, Michael Rusch, Dominik Sigg, Yasmin Vobis, Jeanne Wellinger (project team)

NEW DOCTORATE'S BUILDING NATIONAL UNIVERSITY OF COLOMBIA

Steven Holl (design architect, principal), Chris McVoy (senior partner in charge), Garrick Ambrose, Dimitra Tsachrelia, Alfonso Simelio (project architects), Zach Cohen, Scott Fredricks, Gemma Gene, Johanna Muszbek, Wenying Sun (project team)

INSTITUTE FOR CONTEMPORARY ART, VIRGINIA COMMONWEALTH UNIVERSITY

Steven Holl (design architect, principal), Chris McVoy (senior partner in charge), Dominik Sigg, Dimitra Tsachrelia (project architects), Garrick Ambrose, Rychiee Espinosa, Scott Fredricks, Gary He, Martin Kropac, JongSeo Lee, Yasmin Vobis, Christina Yessios (project team)

MUSEUM OF FINE ARTS HOUSTON CAMPUS EXPANSION

Steven Holl (design architect, principal), Chris McVoy (senior partner in charge), Olaf Schmidt (project architect, senior associate), Filipe Taboada, Yiqing Zhao, Rychiee Espinosa (project architects), Garrick Ambrose, Lourenzo Amaro de Oliveira, Yasmin Bobis, Xi Chen, Carolina Cohen-Freue, JongSeo Lee, Suk Lee, Vaha Markosian, Maki Matsubayashi, Elise Riley, Christopher Rotman, Yun Shi, Alfonso Simelio, Dimitra Tsachrelia, Christina Yessios (project team)

GLASSELL SCHOOL OF ART

Steven Holl (design architect, principal), Chris McVoy (senior partner in charge), Olaf Schmidt (project architect, senior associate), Yiqing Zhao, Rychiee Espinosa, Filipe Taboada (project architects), Xi Chen, Suk Lee, Maki Matsubayashi, Elise Riley, Christopher Rotman, Alfonso Simeo, Yasmin Vobis (project team)

MAGGIE'S CENTRE BARTS

Steven Holl (design architect, principal), Chris McVoy (senior partner in charge), Dominik Sigg (project architect, associate), Bell Cai, Gemma Gene, Martin Kropac, Christina Yessios (project team)

TIANJIN ECO-CITY ECOLOGY AND PLANNING MUSEUMS
Steven Holl (design architect, principal), Roberto Bannura (director in charge), Garrick Ambrose, Michael Rusch (project architects, associates), Yu-Ju Lin (project architect), Chris McVoy (project adviser), Laetitia Buchter, Bell Cai, Xi Chen, Deng Ming Cong, Rychiee Espinosa, Nathalie Frankowski, Annie Kountz, Magdalena Naydekova, Elise Riley, Yun Shi, Wenying Sun, Yasmin Vobis, Manta Weihermann (project team)

JOHN F. KENNEDY CENTER FOR THE PERFORMING ARTS EXPANSION
Steven Holl (design architect, principal), Chris McVoy (senior partner in charge), Garrick Ambrose (project architect, associate), Magdalena Naydekova (assistant project architect), Bell Cai, Kimberly Chew, J. Leehong Kim, Martin Kropac, Elise Riley, Yun Shi, Dominik Sigg, Alfonso Simelio, Yasmin Vobis (project team)

POROSITY PLAN FOR DONGGUAN
Steven Holl (design architect, principal), Garrick Ambrose, Roberto Bannura, Bell Cai, Xi Chen, Annie Kountz, Magdalena Naydekova, Elise Riley (project team)

QINGDAO CULTURE AND ART CENTER
Steven Holl (design architect, principal), Roberto Bannura (project director), Garrick Ambrose, Michael Rusch (associates in charge), Xi Chen (project architect), Noah Yaffe (project adviser), Janine Biunno, Bell Cai, Nathalie Frankowski, Yu-Ju Lin, Magdalena Naydekova, Yun Shi, Wenying Sun, Manta Weihermann, Yiqing Zhao (project team)

TAIWAN CHINPAOSAN NECROPOLIS
Steven Holl (design architect, principal), Roberto Bannura (project director), Noah Yaffe (partner in charge), Xi Chen, Yu-Ju Lin (project architects), Michael Rusch, Bell Cai, Zach Cohen, Yun Shi, Wenying Sun, Yan Zhang (project team)

MUMBAI CITY MUSEUM NORTH WING
Steven Holl (design architect, principal), Noah Yaffe (partner in charge), Chris McVoy (project adviser, senior partner), Yun Shi (project architect), Xi Chen, Michael Haddy, Filipe Taboada (project team)

SHENZHEN LIBRARY AND ART MUSEUM
Steven Holl (design architect, principal), Roberto Bannura (project director), Noah Yaffe (partner in charge), Xi Chen, Yu-Ju Lin (project architects), George Grieves, Jing Han, Yun Shi, Wenying Sun, Yan Zhang (project team)

RUBENSTEIN COMMONS INSTITUTE FOR ADVANCED STUDY
Steven Holl (design architect, principal), Noah Yaffe (partner in charge), Christina Yessios (project architect, associate), Yun Shi (assistant project architect), Marcus Carter, Alessandra Catherine Calaguire (project team), Xi Chen, Carolina Cohen-Freue, Michael Haddy, Elise Riley (competition team)

WINTER VISUAL ARTS CENTER FRANKLIN & MARSHALL COLLEGE
Steven Holl (design architect, principal), Chris McVoy (senior partner in charge), Garrick Ambrose (project architect, associate), Carolina Cohen-Freue (assistant project architect), Dominik Sigg, Marcus Carter, Michael Haddy, Hannah LaSota, Elise Riley (project team)

COFCO CULTURAL AND HEALTH CENTER
Steven Holl (design architect, principal), Roberto Bannura (project director), Noah Yaffe (partner in charge), Xi Chen (project architect), Dimitra Tsachrelia (project adviser), Okki Berendschot, Michael Haddy, Tsung-Yen Hsieh, Lydia Liu, Elise Riley, Yi Ren, Wenying Sun, Ruoyu Wei, Pu Yun, Xu Zhang (project team)

MALAWI LIBRARY AND DORMITORY
Steven Holl (design architect, principal), JongSeo Lee (senior associate in charge), Hannah Ahlblad, Lourenzo Amaro de Oliveira, Okki Berendschot, Suk Lee (project team)

PARACHUTE HYBRIDS TUSHINO DISTRICT

Steven Holl (design architect, principal), Noah Yaffe (partner in charge), Roberto Bannura (director in charge), Marcus Carter (project architect), Lourenzo Amaro de Oliveira, Michael Haddy, Seo Hee Lee, Suk Lee, Aleksandr Plotkin, Yun Shi, Wenying Sun, Ruoyu Wei, Yiqing Zhao (project team)

GARE DU NORD

Steven Holl (design architect, principal), Chris McVoy (partner in charge), Filipe Taboada (project architect, associate), Michael Haddy, Seo Hee Lee, Jacobo Mingorance Arranz (project team)

MÉDECINS SANS FRONTIÈRES HEADQUARTERS

Steven Holl (design architect, principal), Noah Yaffe (partner in charge), Ruoyu Wei, Whitney Forward (project architects), Alfonso Simelio, Filipe Taboada (project team)

IMAGINE ANGERS COLLECTORS MUSEUM AND HOTEL

Steven Holl (design architect, principal), Noah Yaffe (partner in charge), Alessandra Catherine Calaguire, Ruoyu Wei (project team)

ARCHITECTURE ARCHIVE AND RESEARCH LIBRARY

Steven Holl (design architect, principal), Dimitra Tsachrelia (project architect, associate), Ruoyu Wei (assistant project architect), António Costa Almeida, Paul H. Hazelet (project team)

UNIVERSITY COLLEGE DUBLIN FUTURE CAMPUS EXTENSION

Steven Holl (design architect, principal), Chris McVoy (senior partner in charge), Filipe Taboada (project architect, associate), Ruoyu Wei (project architect), Alessandra Catherine Calaguire, Michael Haddy, Seo Hee Lee, Jacobo Mingorance Arranz (project team)

CIFI OFFICE BUILDING

Steven Holl (design architect, principal), Roberto Bannura (partner in charge), Chris McVoy (adviser, senior partner), Yuanchu Yi, Yiqing Zhao, Yun Shi (project architects), Yangyang Xu, Jinxin Ma, Shih Hsueh Wang, Seo Hee Lee (project team)

OSTRAVA CONCERT HALL

Steven Holl (design architect, principal), Dimitra Tsachrelia (project architect, associate), Lirong Tan, Paul H. Hazelet (project team)

IMAGE CREDITS

All images © Steven Holl / Steven Holl Architects, except for the following:

Adobe Stock 117 top left, 121, 159 top right
Garrick Ambrose 109 top
Iwan Baan 36, 39 top left and bottom, 40, 43, 50, 53 top left, 57, 58, 66, 68, 71, 80, 85, 94, 97, 99
Richard Barnes 90, 93
BNIM 109 bottom
Chapel of St. Ignatius 19
Field Condition 109 bottom
Steen Gyldendal 39 top right
Paul Klee 30 bottom
Chris McVoy 53 top right, 61 top, 108
Thomas Molvig 7 right
Todd Rosenberg 164
Filipe Taboada 48 top left
Dimitra Tsachrelia 15
Salk Institute for Biological Studies 10
Paul Warchol 18, 22, 44, 48 top center, top right, and bottom, 154 bottom
Susan Wides 6, 7 left, 17, 21, 28, 53 bottom
Christina Yessios 129 bottom

ACKNOWLEDGMENTS

Princeton Architectural Press has been, from the beginning, a special patron for our works. We deeply appreciate the dedication of Kevin Lippert, Jennifer Lippert, and their staff in our effort toward Architecture. Collaboration—the main engine underlying the realization of inspiring architecture—is essential in each one of these projects. As they span a period of three decades, the individuals who dedicated themselves are listed in the project credits according to each building.

The collaborative efforts so crucial to realizing architecture are likewise essential to realizing a book. Here, Connor Stankard acted as an editor and graphic designer. The enthusiastic support and editing from Dimitra Tsachrelia is a blessing of fundamental importance. Molly Blieden's sustained dedication continues into its twenty-sixth year. The artists Mike Metz, Lars Müller, Fer Felder, and many others offered valuable critique. The help of Enrique Garcia and Paul Hazelet is deeply appreciated.

Published by
Princeton Architectural Press
202 Warren Street
Hudson, NY 12534
www.papress.com

Printed in China
22 21 20 19 4 3 2 1 First edition

Editor: Sara Stemen
Designer: Steven Holl Office with PAPress

Special thanks to:
Paula Baver, Janet Behning, Abby Bussel, Jan Cigliano Hartman, Susan Hershberg, Stephanie Holstein, Kristen Hewitt, Lia Hunt, Valerie Kamen, Jennifer Lippert, Sara McKay, Parker Menzimer, Wes Seeley, Rob Shaeffer, Jessica Tackett, Marisa Tesoro, Paul Wagner, and Joseph Weston of Princeton Architectural Press
—Kevin C. Lippert, publisher

Library of Congress Cataloging-in-Publication Data
Names: Holl, Steven, author.
Title: Compression / Steven Holl.
Description: First edition. | New York : Princeton Architectural Press, 2019.
Identifiers: LCCN 2019006450 | ISBN 9781616898519 (hardcover : alk. paper)
Subjects: LCSH: Holl, Steven—Themes, motives. | Steven Holl Architects.
Classification: LCC NA737.H56 A4 2019 | DDC 720.92—dc23
LC record available at
https://lccn.loc.gov/2019006450